DAVID FARRAGUT

AND THE GREAT NAVAL BLOCKADE

THE HISTORY OF THE CIVIL WAR

THE HISTORY OF THE CIVIL WAR

DAVID FARRAGUT

AND THE GREAT NAVAL BLOCKADE

by RUSSELL SHORTO

INTRODUCTORY ESSAY BY
HENRY STEELE COMMAGER

SILVER BURDETT PRESS

Series Editorial Supervisor: Richard G. Gallin
Series Editing: Agincourt Press
Series Consultant: Elizabeth Fortson
Cover and Text Design: Circa 86, New York
Series Supervision of Art and Design: Leslie Bauman
Maps: Susan Johnston Carlson

Consultants: Rudy Johnson, Social Studies Coordinator, Lansing
Public Schools, Lansing, Michigan; Frank de Varona, Associate
Superintendent, Dade County Public Schools, Dade County, Florida.

Library of Congress Cataloging-in-Publication Data
Shorto, Russell.
    David Farragut and the great naval blockade / by Russell Shorto.
      p.   cm. — (The history of the Civil War)
    Includes bibliograpical references (p. 123).
    Summary: A biography of the American Naval officer for whom Congress created the
rank of full admiral for his service in the Civil War.
    1. Farragut, David Glasgow, 1801-1870—Juvenile literature. 2. Admirals—United
States—Biography—Juvenile literature. 3. United States. Navy—Biography—Juvenile
Literature. 4. United States—History—Civil War, 1861-1865—Naval operations—Juvenile
literature. 5. United States—History—Civil War, 1861-1865—Blockades—Juvenile
literature. 6. United States—History—Civil War, 1861-1865—Naval operations. [1.
Farragut, David Glasgow, 1801-1870. 2. Admirals.] I. Title. II. Series.
E467.1.F23S35   1990
973.7'S'092—dc20
[B]
[92]   90-32367
ISBN 0-382-09941-9 (lib. bdg.)   ISBN 0-382-24050-2 (pbk.)   CIP
                                                AC

TABLE OF CONTENTS

Born in land-locked Tennessee, David Farragut spent most of his life at sea. When he was very young his family moved to New Orleans, where both his father and brother enlisted in the navy. Farragut's mother helped care for Captain David Porter, who had fought briefly in the wars with France and the Barbary pirates. With the onset of the War of 1812 with Britain, Porter—now a commodore—took young Farragut as a midshipman in the new American navy. From that time—and for more than half a century—David Farragut lived in and for the navy.

Farragut sailed with Porter on a famous voyage around Cape Horn and more than halfway across the Pacific. Together, they discovered a group of islands that was not yet on any map—islands that they promptly annexed to the United States and named the Madison Islands after the American president. Young Farragut—just 12 years old—was put in charge of one of Porter's ships, sailed it back to South America and fought in a fierce battle against two British ships then refitting at Valparaiso, Chile.

After that, young David was shipped off to the Mediterrean, where he managed to acquire experience on three well-named ships: The *Franklin*, the *Washington*, and the *Independence*. He also acquired three languages: Spanish, Italian, and Arabic. A lieutenant now, he devoted himself to "routine" duties such as driving pirates out of the Caribbean and protecting American interests at Tampico and Vera Cruz during the war between Mexico and France. It was all dull enough to a sailor who had already fought halfway around the globe before his 15th birthday.

But the most stirring chapters of Farragut's life were still ahead—with the outbreak of the Civil War. Farragut had been born in Tennessee and lived in Virginia, but when war was announced he promptly packed his bags and headed north. His allegiance was to the flag he sailed under, not to the soil he lived on.

If the North was to win the Civil War and save the Union, it had to cut off military and other supplies being sent to the Confederacy by Britain and France. This strategy called for a successful blockade of the South. Since not every port in the South could be blockaded at once, it was necessary to single out and attack the few strategic ports where blockade runners were successful. These ports were New Orleans, Galveston, Charleston, and Mobile Bay. Farragut, by this time a senior officer in the U.S. Navy, was selected by President Lincoln to lead the attack on these ports. The first task was to open the Mississippi River at New Orleans. Then it would be necessary to sail north and help General Ulysses S. Grant conquer Vicksburg, where he would engage in a land battle with help from Farragut's gunboats.

Farragut knew better than anyone that if the Union were to survive, it would have to depend on its navy. The navy had not fought a real war since the War of 1812. But, despite the dangers, Farragut decided to run the blockade and risk the torpedos. Lashing himself to the rigging, he commanded the whole of his fleet from the top of a mast. When he heard the warning cry "Torpedos ahead!" Farragut's response was historic: "Damn the torpedos! Full speed ahead!"

CIVIL WAR TIME LINE

May 22
Kansas-Nebraska Act states that in new territories the question of slavery will be decided by the citizens. Many Northerners are outraged because this act could lead to the extension of slavery.

| 1854 | 1855 | 1856 | 1857 |

May 21
Lawrence, Kansas is sacked by proslavery Missourians.
May 22
Senator Charles Sumner is caned by Preston Brooks for delivering a speech against slavery.
May 24 – 25
Pottawatomie Creek massacre committed by John Brown and four of his sons.

March 6
The Supreme Court, in the *Dred Scott* ruling, declares that blacks are not U. S. citizens, and therefore cannot bring lawsuits. The ruling divides the country on the question of the legal status of blacks.

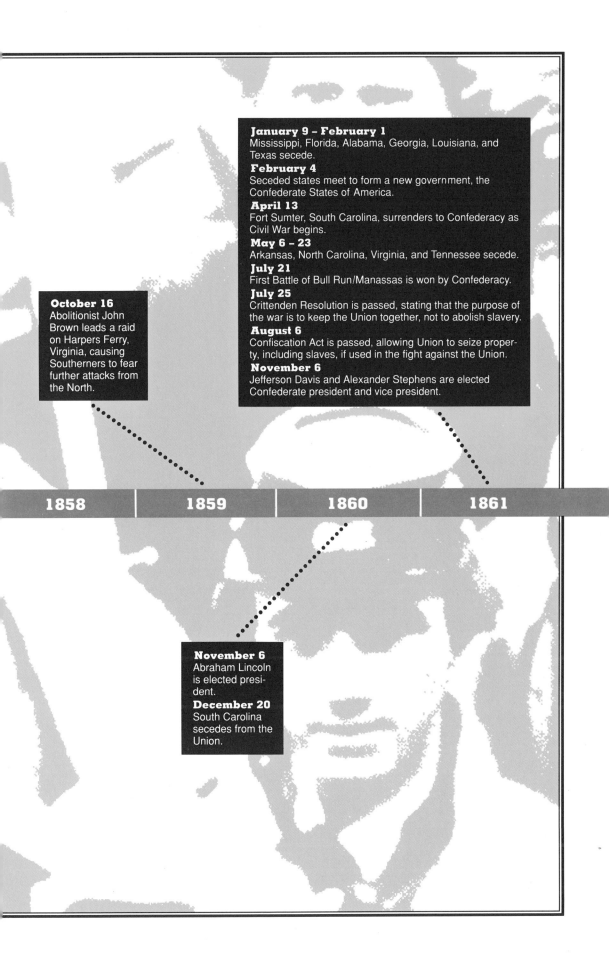

January 9 – February 1
Mississippi, Florida, Alabama, Georgia, Louisiana, and Texas secede.
February 4
Seceded states meet to form a new government, the Confederate States of America.
April 13
Fort Sumter, South Carolina, surrenders to Confederacy as Civil War begins.
May 6 – 23
Arkansas, North Carolina, Virginia, and Tennessee secede.
July 21
First Battle of Bull Run/Manassas is won by Confederacy.
July 25
Crittenden Resolution is passed, stating that the purpose of the war is to keep the Union together, not to abolish slavery.
August 6
Confiscation Act is passed, allowing Union to seize property, including slaves, if used in the fight against the Union.
November 6
Jefferson Davis and Alexander Stephens are elected Confederate president and vice president.

October 16
Abolitionist John Brown leads a raid on Harpers Ferry, Virginia, causing Southerners to fear further attacks from the North.

1858   **1859**   **1860**   **1861**

November 6
Abraham Lincoln is elected president.
December 20
South Carolina secedes from the Union.

February 6
Fort Henry, Tennessee, is captured.

February 16
Fort Donelson, Tennessee, is captured by Union.

March 9
Monitor and *Merrimack* battle near Hampton Roads, Virginia.

March 23
Shenandoah Valley Campaign opens with Union victory over Maj. Gen. Thomas J. "Stonewall" Jackson.

April 7
Gen. Ulysses S. Grant wins Battle of Shiloh, Tennessee, splitting rebel forces on the Mississippi River.

April 25
New Orleans is captured by Union naval forces led by flag officer David Farragut.

June 19
Slavery is abolished in U. S. territories.

June 25
Gen. Robert E. Lee leads rout of Gen. George McClellan's army in the Seven Days Battles.

July 17
The United States Congress authorizes formation of the first black regiments.

August 29 – 30
Second Battle of Bull Run/Manassas is won by Confederacy.

September 5
Lee leads first Confederate invasion of the North into Maryland.

September 17
Battle of Antietam/Sharpsburg, bloodiest of the war, ends in a stalemate between Lee and McClellan.

1862   **1863**   **1864**   **1865**

January 1
Lincoln issues Emancipation Proclamation, freeing slaves in Confederate states.

March 3
U.S. Congress passes its first military draft.

April 2
Bread riots occur in Richmond, Virginia.

May 1 – 4
Battle of Chancellorsville is won by Confederacy; Stonewall Jackson is accidentally shot by his own troops.

May 22 – July 4
Union wins siege of Vicksburg in Mississippi.

June 3
Lee invades the North from Fredericksburg, Virginia.

July 3
Battle of Gettysburg is won in Pennsylvania by Union.

July 13 – 17
Riots occur in New York City over the draft.

November 19
Lincoln delivers the Gettysburg Address.

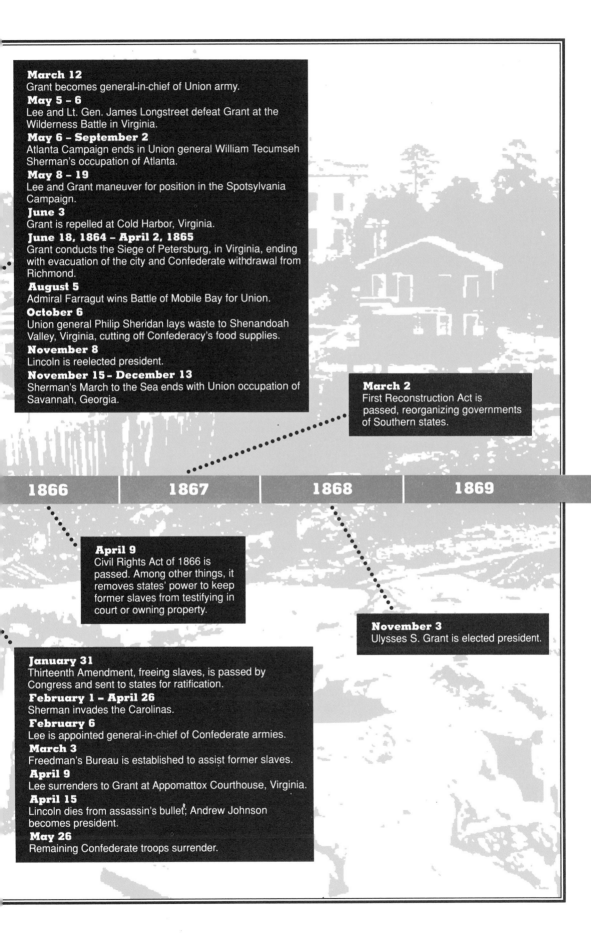

March 12
Grant becomes general-in-chief of Union army.
May 5 – 6
Lee and Lt. Gen. James Longstreet defeat Grant at the Wilderness Battle in Virginia.
May 6 – September 2
Atlanta Campaign ends in Union general William Tecumseh Sherman's occupation of Atlanta.
May 8 – 19
Lee and Grant maneuver for position in the Spotsylvania Campaign.
June 3
Grant is repelled at Cold Harbor, Virginia.
June 18, 1864 – April 2, 1865
Grant conducts the Siege of Petersburg, in Virginia, ending with evacuation of the city and Confederate withdrawal from Richmond.
August 5
Admiral Farragut wins Battle of Mobile Bay for Union.
October 6
Union general Philip Sheridan lays waste to Shenandoah Valley, Virginia, cutting off Confederacy's food supplies.
November 8
Lincoln is reelected president.
November 15 – December 13
Sherman's March to the Sea ends with Union occupation of Savannah, Georgia.

March 2
First Reconstruction Act is passed, reorganizing governments of Southern states.

1866 **1867** **1868** **1869**

April 9
Civil Rights Act of 1866 is passed. Among other things, it removes states' power to keep former slaves from testifying in court or owning property.

November 3
Ulysses S. Grant is elected president.

January 31
Thirteenth Amendment, freeing slaves, is passed by Congress and sent to states for ratification.
February 1 – April 26
Sherman invades the Carolinas.
February 6
Lee is appointed general-in-chief of Confederate armies.
March 3
Freedman's Bureau is established to assist former slaves.
April 9
Lee surrenders to Grant at Appomattox Courthouse, Virginia.
April 15
Lincoln dies from assassin's bullet; Andrew Johnson becomes president.
May 26
Remaining Confederate troops surrender.

DESTINED FOR THE SEA

"I soon became fond of this adventurous sort of life."

ADMIRAL FARRAGUT, ON HIS EARLY LIFE AT SEA

One day in 1808, a Louisiana farmer did something that would change the course of American naval history: he went fishing. The man, George Farragut, was a former sailor who lived on the shores of Lake Pontchartrain, just north of New Orleans. He was out on the lake in his log canoe when he came upon another boat that seemed to be unmanned. Coming closer, Farragut found a man lying unconscious on the deck. He recognized the man as David Porter, an acquaintance from the naval station at New Orleans.

George Farragut brought the man to the rambling house on the shores of the lake where he and his family lived. His young son, James Glasgow, who was called Glasgow, and his wife, Elizabeth, rushed to help. Porter was an old man, and had been in poor health for some years. When he eventually regained consciousness, the family learned that he had been overcome by sunstroke on the boat. Elizabeth Farragut nursed him for several days until, quite suddenly, she herself became ill. Now seven-year-old Glasgow took over caring for the old man. His younger brother George helped. Soon it was determined that their mother had yellow fever, a dread disease common in the swampy bayous of Louisiana.

In one terrible week, both David Porter and Elizabeth Farragut died. A joint funeral was held, and they were buried on the same day.

The sudden loss of their mother stunned the Farragut children. For several months the little family struggled on. George Farragut grieved for his wife and wondered how he would cope without her. He had met her in Tennessee, when he was a naval officer working as an agent of the U.S. government. Elizabeth Shine had moved with her family from North Carolina to Tennessee. She was 10 years younger than George Farragut. She fell in love with the dashing officer, married him, and began raising a family. They moved to Louisiana when George was appointed to the naval station in New Orleans.

And now this tragedy. Elizabeth was gone, and George had to cope on his own. His oldest son, William, was away in the navy, so he was taken care of. But in addition to Glasgow and George, he had two very young daughters, Nancy and Elizabeth. When a

neighbor offered to take them in and care for them, George Farragut felt he had no choice.

One day soon afterward, the family received a visitor. He was tall, broad-chested, and dressed magnificently in a navy uniform. His jacket was blue, with brass buttons and shiny gold epaulets, or shoulder fringes. He was Commander David Porter, son of the old man whom they had cared for.

Commander Porter said he had come because he felt deeply grateful to George Farragut for making his father's last days as comfortable as possible. In return for the family's kindness, he told Mr. Farragut that he would like to take young Glasgow with him and train him to be a naval officer.

Father and son discussed the offer. It was not unusual in those days for parents to have a child or several of their children "adopted" by someone who could train them in a career. And since Commander Porter was stationed nearby in New Orleans, Glasgow could still visit his father.

George Farragut liked the idea, for he was a navy man himself. He was Spanish, born on the island of Minorca, off the east coast of Spain. His ancestors, stretching far back into the Middle Ages, were sailors and fighting men. One of his ancestors, Don Pedro Ferregut, a nobleman of the Middle Ages, fought heroically at the side of James I, king of Aragon, in 1229. In the 17th century, Captain Antonio Ferregut served in the navy during the reign of King Philip IV. Other ancestors included bishops, councilors, and scholars.

George himself had gone to school in Barcelona, Spain, then traveled to America as captain of a trading ship. He arrived in 1776, just as the Revolutionary War broke out. He became swept up in the revolutionary spirit and immediately decided to fight on the side of the colonists.

Ferregut served in the South Carolina navy, fighting valiantly for his new country. He faced the British in battles at Savannah, Georgia, and South Carolina, before he was captured. He escaped, and soon after fought with distinction in the Continental army. In one battle, his right arm bone was shattered by a bullet. By the end of the war, he had reached the rank of major of the cavalry.

After the war, he settled in Campbell's Station, Tennessee. In the Spanish style, his name was spelled Jorge Ferregut, but once he settled in the United States, he Americanized the spelling to George Farragut. In Tennessee he became a local militiaman, guarding the frontier. Two sons were born there. Then came his appointment to the naval base in New Orleans.

George Farragut was devoted to the United States, his adopted country, and to the life of the sea. Still, he let his son make the choice about his own future.

Glasgow did not have to think long. The year was 1808. The United States of America was a very young country, with many potential enemies. The tiny navy would grow quickly in the years to come and the nation would have great need of skilled officers. Glasgow's older brother was already a midshipman in the navy. He knew that his father had served in the navy with great honor, and Glasgow admired him above anyone. He would accept Commander Porter's offer.

So began a career that would span almost six decades. James Glasgow Farragut, who would soon change his name to David in honor of his adopted father, David Porter, would rise to become the most outstanding naval officer in the history of his young country, the first man to be awarded the rank of admiral of the navy. Although his most famous victories would come near the end of his career, during the American Civil War, he would not have to wait that long for adventure. Another war was fast approaching, and the boy would see action before he was even a teenager.

David Farragut (as he soon began calling himself) moved into Commander Porter's house in New Orleans in 1809, when he was eight years old. The two liked each other from the start. David always wanted to hear about his guardian's brave and daring deeds. Porter had fought against the French and was once captured by pirates in Tripoli. Commander Porter, for his part, was generous and kind, always interested in furthering David's education.

In New Orleans, a whole new world opened up for young David. He had been born in a remote area of Tennessee. His family had moved to Louisiana when David was not much more than a

baby. Most of his young life had been spent among the tropical palmetto trees and moss-covered oaks along the banks of Lake Pontchartrain. His family and a few neighbors were the only people he had ever seen.

New Orleans could not have been more different. It was a bustling city of 15,000 people, and growing fast. It was only five and a half years before, in 1803, that President Thomas Jefferson had bought Louisiana from France for about $15 million, doubling the area of the United States. Both France and Spain had owned the Louisiana Territory, which extended from the Gulf of Mexico to Canada, and from the Mississippi River to the Rocky Mountains. France had owned it until 1763, when it yielded it to Spain. Spain then ruled the territory for almost 40 years. The French ruler Napoleon Bonaparte forced Spain to give it back to France. Shortly afterward France sold it to the United States. This vast territory was to become 13 future states, and the greatest city of the territory was New Orleans.

Highlights in the Life of David Farragut

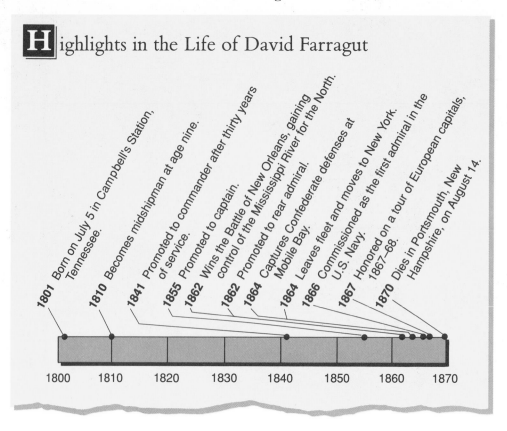

1801 Born on July 5 in Campbell's Station, Tennessee.

1810 Becomes midshipman at age nine.

1841 Promoted to commander after thirty years of service.

1855 Promoted to captain.

1862 Wins the Battle of New Orleans, gaining control of the Mississippi River for the North.

1862 Promoted to rear admiral.

1864 Captures Confederate defenses at Mobile Bay.

1864 Leaves fleet and moves to New York.

1866 Commissioned as the first admiral in the U.S. Navy.

1867 Honored on a tour of European capitals, 1867–68.

1870 Dies in Portsmouth, New Hampshire, on August 14.

1800 1810 1820 1830 1840 1850 1860 1870

The people of New Orleans were a mixture of rich and poor, who spoke French, Spanish, and English. The broad avenues were lined with the mansions of the rich, and winding alleyways, reeking of sewage, were home to the masses of poor people. Many houses reflected the Spanish influence, with red tiled roofs, wide verandas, and ornate metal gates. It was an eyeful for the eight-year-old boy.

New Orleans was a natural as a base for naval operations. At that time rivers were the great highways that served the nation, carrying all manner of goods on huge flatboats. They were also strategically important, because control of the rivers meant control of much of the land. New Orleans was located at the southern end of the greatest river on the continent, the mighty Mississippi.

The 13 states along the East Coast relied on ships sailing along the coast for trade, and on the crude roads. But in the western territories the Mississippi River was the most important means of transportation and communication. Goods were shipped along the river, and all news came by way of the Mississippi as well. The Mississippi was everyone's link to the outside world.

From Louisiana in the south, to Illinois in the north, the river kept the western territories together. Without communication of some kind there was no way that settlers in places as far away as Louisiana and Indiana or Illinois would even have felt they were part of the same country. It was also possible to travel up from New Orleans to where the Mississippi joined the Ohio River. From there, boats could travel eastward as far as Pittsburgh. In this way the western lands were connected with events in the East. Because of the river network, New Orleans and Pittsburgh—which were more than a thousand miles apart—could keep in touch with each other.

New Orleans was an important port for another reason, too. It was located on the Gulf of Mexico. This was the perfect place for boats carrying cargo from Europe and South and Central America to dock. It was sheltered and generally warm throughout the year so sailors never had to worry about being delayed by ice and frozen channels.

Since the city was such an important center of shipping, it was full of naval officers, dock workers, and sailors from many countries. It was also a haven for pirates. Although slavery was still legal, importing slaves from other countries was no longer legal after 1807. But many plantation owners in the South were willing to pay high prices to those who found a way to bring in slaves from the Caribbean islands (then called the West Indies). The pirates found ways of doing this and they made huge amounts of money in the illegal slave trade. The most famous and treacherous of these pirates were the brothers Jean and Pierre Lafitte.

David Farragut spent the next few months living with Commander Porter on the New Orleans naval base. Though he had no formal schooling during this period, he began his education as a sailor by getting hands-on experience. Commander Porter was assigned to track down some pirates reported to be on the Mississippi, and David went along. It was an exciting start to a career at sea.

Soon after the expedition, Commander Porter determined that there were no proper schools in New Orleans for David to attend. Since he had to travel to Washington, D.C. on naval business, he decided to bring David with him.

David Farragut's first open-sea voyage was from New Orleans to Washington. Their vessel was the bomb ketch *Vesuvius*, a ship with masts fore and aft and 11 guns along the sides. When this ship set sail, David stood on the deck and watched as the sails were set, and thrilled as they billowed in the wind.

Commander David Porter brought David Farragut into the U.S. Navy at age nine.

The first port of call was Havana, Cuba, where Commander Porter dropped off the band of French pirates he had caught and claimed his reward. Not yet nine years old, David Farragut, sailor, set foot on foreign soil. He listened to people on the docks, watched sugar cane being loaded onto boats, basked in the hot sun, and enjoyed himself very much.

He heard some unsettling stories. There were troubles in the seas between the United States and England. England and France were at war, and England badly needed sailors. So English ships were stopping American vessels and searching them in order to find any British subjects who might be aboard. Sometimes American sailors were taken by force by the British officers, who claimed they had been born in England. The Americans considered this a violation of the freedom of the seas and of international law, as well as an invasion of American property. American seamen were especially up in arms about it.

Young David Farragut had heard stories about the Revolutionary War from his father. He knew that England and America had been enemies in the past. Now they would be enemies once more. On the docks of Havana, American sailors were hotly discussing the ship *Vixen*, which had been fired on by a British ship trying to board it. "This was the first thing that caused in me bad feeling toward the English nation," David later wrote in his journal. "I looked upon this as an insult to be paid in kind, and was anxious to discharge the debt with interest."

He would soon get a chance, for the two nations were drifting steadily toward war. Meanwhile, David and Commander Porter made their way to Washington, where the boy was enrolled in school. He studied military tactics as well as the more usual school subjects. Here, also, Commander Porter introduced him to the secretary of the navy, Paul Hamilton.

David was awed by the important man, his spacious office, and his magnificent uniform. But he answered questions sharply, as a would-be officer ought to. The secretary looked sternly at David and asked if he was sure he wanted a career in the navy. David said he was quite sure. So the secretary promised that when David turned 10 he would personally issue him a midshipman's warrant. This document would make him an official sailor.

David left the office delighted, and counted down the months to his tenth birthday. He did not have to wait long. The warrant arrived early, in December 1810. David Farragut was now a midshipman in the United States Navy, an officer-in-training who would soon see action in the War of 1812. He was nine-and-a-half years old.

THE VOYAGE OF THE "ESSEX"

"He was the life of the midshipman's mess, full of
fun and agile as a cat."

RICHARD B. PORTER,
GRANDSON OF THE CAPTAIN, ON YOUNG FARRAGUT

I t was the Fourth of July. Guns fired, sailors whooped and
cheered, and the Stars and Stripes flapped high overhead.
The crew of the frigate *Essex* was having a party.

It was their first full day at sea, and Captain Porter had
encouraged the holiday celebration. They were on their way to join
forces with the squadron under the command of Commodore John
Rodgers. Their mission was to attack British merchant ships and
damage England's commerce.

Only 16 days before, on June 18, 1812, the Congress, following
President James Madison's request, had formally declared war on
England. The War of 1812 had begun. David Porter had been
promoted to captain and given command of the *Essex*. And the
youngest midshipman aboard—indeed, the youngest in the whole
navy—was the slim, dark-haired, 11-year-old David Farragut.

The crew would soon face the horrors of war, but for now
Captain Porter allowed them a celebration. He ordered an extra
measure of grog (rum and water) to be given to each sailor, and
after dinner everyone got an extra helping of "duff," or plum
pudding. Captain Porter wanted his crew to honor their country's

birth, and to remember what it stood for, as they went off to fight for it.

Why did they decide to fight? There were many causes for the war. Bad feelings had been building for many years between the former colony and its parent country. England considered the new United States government too unstable to manage so large an area. Nevertheless, many Americans wanted even more land. They wanted to expand into Canada, which was a territory controlled by England. Another reason was that England was still at war with France, and British warships regularly raided American merchant vessels for men or supplies. This was illegal, a violation of both international law and the idea of freedom of the seas. But the United States was still too weak to do anything about it. Finally, Congress was forced to declare war.

David Farragut, as he stood on the deck with his mates cheering the holiday and the voyage, understood only vaguely the causes of the war. He knew much more clearly his immediate circumstances. He had learned the *Essex* inside and out. He knew its ropes and stays, the quality of its rigging and the height of its mast. He could tie any knot you could name. He knew the importance of keeping loose running gear neatly coiled on the deck. The blood of a sailor flowed in his veins.

He also knew his duties and carried them out well. As a midshipman—an officer in training—he was responsible for passing along the orders of the officers as they were barked from the quarterdeck. He helped keep the watch at night. He supervised the rationing of supplies to the men. And most important, he had to be ever on the alert to do what the captain ordered.

Rationing supplies was a vital task, he soon learned. The most precious supply was water. Not long after the crew had been gathered, David became friends with the boatswain's mate (the man in charge of the deck crew), a salty old dog named William Kingsbury. Farragut later wrote that, soon after the *Essex* set sail, Kingsbury said to him: "Mr. Farragut, it don't take more than a week on a cruise when the water ain't fit to drink. Why, sir, it gets as dark-colored as the captain's mahogany table, and all full of wrigglers, and it fair stinks!'' The best that could be done to improve the water in those days was to mix it with rum, which would kill some of the foul taste.

Young David Farragut found everything thrilling during those first weeks at sea. When he was not on duty he scampered all over the deck or crawled out on the yardarms, poles that stuck out from the square mainsail. Even during mess (the ship's meals), he was lively. "He was the life of the midshipmen's mess [table]," Captain Porter's grandson said many years later, "full of fun and agile as a cat. He liked nothing better than to climb to the top of the mainmast and sit curl-legged, gazing out to sea."

He found even the hardships at sea interesting at first. In winter there was no efficient way to heat the steerage, where the midshipmen slept in their hammocks. On the coldest nights the best they could do was to use "hot shot." This was a cannonball heated red-hot in the ovens of the galley, set into a bucket of sand.

David had some friends among the other midshipmen, including Jack Cowan and Henry Ogden, both slightly older than he. The youths would sit around the glowing ball warming their hands and feet as best they could.

The *Essex* was a fine ship, as the crew well knew. "The *Essex* is rated a 32-gun frigate, but mounts 44," wrote her purser, or money officer, Melancton Bostwick, at the start of the voyage, "and carries about 350 men, as eager for a skirmish with the British as any set of men you ever saw."

Farragut, later in life, also had something to say about the *Essex* and her crew: "We cruised on the coast, and exercised the crews until they were brought to as great a state of perfection and discipline as ever existed, perhaps, in the Navy," he wrote. "Our ship, the *Essex*, was the 'smartest' in the squadron, and Commodore Rodgers complimented our captain highly."

The United States Navy owned a few more fine ships like the *Essex*, but "a few" were not enough to tackle the British fleet, which was the most powerful in the world. England ruled the seven seas. The British navy had 600 warships in its fleet. The American navy had 16. It was an absurdly one-sided struggle, and nobody really expected the Americans to last, including the American leaders themselves. In fact, for some time all American warships were kept in port so that forts along the coast could protect them.

Finally, though, President James Madison became convinced that the ships would have to do their best against the British fleet that was blockading the coast. It was as though the British ships were imprisoning the country. Ships like the *Essex* had to break out and cause trouble elsewhere to divert the mighty British navy. That was their job.

The *Essex* managed to slip past the line of British ships that patrolled the coast. It then set out single-handedly to destroy the enemy's trade. In a span of two months the *Essex* captured eight British merchant ships loaded with cargo. Never once did the ship enter into battle, for the merchant ships surrendered when they saw a fully equipped warship bearing down on them.

Midshipman Farragut's first assignment was aboard the U.S.S. *Essex*.

Then, in August of 1812, Midshipman Farragut got his first taste of battle. The *Essex*, still on its own, came upon a 20-gun British sloop of war, the *Alert*. (A war sloop was a warship with all of its guns mounted on the deck. A frigate like the *Essex* had guns mounted on a lower level also.) The *Essex* flew the British flag, called the Union Jack, in order to trick the enemy. The *Alert* came up to investigate. Captain Porter ordered his men to turn the ship as though it were about to flee. But he also sent the men to battle stations and ordered the guns primed and readied.

Then, with the *Alert* just behind them, close enough for Midshipman Farragut to hear the shouts of their crew as they got into position, Porter had the Union Jack taken down and the Stars and Stripes raised. Suddenly a great cheer went up on the *Alert*. The British sailors were happy to have an American prize delivered to them so neatly. They fired their guns, but they were shooting at a bad angle, so the shells only bounced off the sides of the *Essex*.

Then they fired a broadside of "grape and canister." This was a shotgunlike blast that was intended to rain down on the crew. But again the angle was off. Porter now knew he had them. He brought the *Essex* around and fired his guns. For eight minutes the *Essex's* cannons bombarded the *Alert*. In the end, the Union Jack came down on the *Alert*, the sign that it was ready to surrender. The *Essex* had won its first sea battle. Midshipman Farragut had tasted the bitter grit of gunpowder in the air, heard the excited cries of men in battle, and had performed admirably.

But the story of the *Alert* was not over. After the battle, the crew of the *Essex* repaired the ship they had damaged and towed it. They brought the *Alert's* officers into their hold as prisoners, while the British crew stayed on board their own ship.

One night David Farragut lay sleeping in his hammock when he felt someone leaning over him in the darkness. He opened his eyes just enough to see one of the officers of the *Alert* holding a pistol and peering down at him. David quickly shut his eyes again and breathed as though he were sound asleep. In a few minutes the officer stole out of the steerage.

As soon as he was gone, David was up and hurrying silently to the captain's quarters. The prisoners were attempting an escape! The boy told Captain Porter what had just happened. The captain thought for a moment. If he rang the alarm the prisoners—whom he knew were armed—would begin shooting. Instead he ran up on deck and began crying:

"Fire! Fire!"

Captain Porter ran a tight ship, and one of the things he made the crew practice over and over again was the fire drill. He had even started small fires to lead his men to believe there was the threat of a real fire. As a result, the crew of the *Essex* was the most efficient in the navy at responding to a fire drill. Instantly the officers and sailors streamed onto the deck and raced into position. Each man had a blanket over his shoulder and a sword in his hand, following drill procedures. As they came on deck they realized the true situation. The only people confused by what was going on were the prisoners. In a matter of moments the crew had them locked up tight down in the ship's hold. This time they made sure there would be no more escape attempts.

Disaster was avoided thanks to the quick action of David Farragut. It was his first heroic act at sea. It would not be his last.

After the adventure with the *Alert*, Captain Porter planned to head back to port for more food and supplies. When the ship sailed into Delaware Bay, however, the captain was angered to find that there were no supplies there. The government had decided to reoutfit the *Essex* for a long voyage. Captain Porter had no choice but to head inland to anchor for a complete refitting.

On September 15, 1812, the *Essex* sailed up the Delaware River. It had been 10 weeks of high adventure for 11-year-old David Farragut. But this was not the end. The war had not yet entered its bloodiest phase. The *Essex* had more work to do.

ADVENTURE IN THE PACIFIC

"I felt no little pride in finding myself in
command at twelve years of age."

DAVID FARRAGUT

I n October the *Essex*, which had been docked on the
Delaware River, again set sail in search of British merchant
ships. It headed across the Atlantic to the Cape Verde
Islands, off the west coast of Africa. There the *Essex* would meet up
with the ships in Commodore Bainbridge's squadron.

This plan was created to evade the British warships, called men-
of-war, which would be lying in wait for them. From there the
squadron would proceed southwest across the Atlantic to the
isolated island of Fernando de Noronha, off the northeast coast of
Brazil. They would then travel south all the way around Cape
Horn, at the southern tip of South America, and head for the South
Pacific Ocean, where British boats were fishing peacefully. Their
objective: to destroy the British whaling industry.

Another reason the ships had to travel this roundabout route was
that there was no other sea lane. The Panama Canal would not be
cut across the narrow isthmus of Panama for many years. Ships
sailing from the Atlantic to the Pacific at this time had to sail all the
way around South America.

When the *Essex* reached the Cape Verde Islands in November 1812, there was still no sign of the other ships it was to meet. The *Essex* waited five days, then set off for the next meeting point off the coast of Brazil. Still no sign of Bainbridge's ships. Instead, the *Essex* encountered a British packet ship (a passenger boat carrying mail and cargo), the *Nocton*, which carried $55,000 in hard currency on board. The *Essex* easily captured the British ship.

At this point Captain Porter made a bold decision: The *Essex* would voyage into the Pacific alone, using the money taken from the *Nocton* to fund its adventure. Using money stolen from the enemy was common practice. The sailors, always devoted to their captain, shouted their approval of his plan. The *Essex* was off on one of the most daring and exciting exploits of the war.

Down the coast of South America the *Essex* traveled, sails billowing in the stiff winds. Cape Horn, at the tip of the continent, is always rough and stormy. Fierce winds whip around the Cape from the west, causing any ship coming from the east severe hardship. The *Essex* was tossed about for 21 days. The crew fought the savage winds and high walls of water, day in and day out, until their bones ached and they felt they could no longer go on.

At one point the seas were tossing so violently that the ship came close to turning over. While it was nearly on its side, a great wall of water came crashing in. Waves swept over the deck. The gun ports filled with water. Sailors cried out, fearing they were sinking.

Years later, Admiral Farragut remembered his first terrible storm at sea:

"This was the only instance in which I ever saw a real good seaman paralyzed by fear at the dangers of the sea. Several of the sailors were seen on their knees at prayer, but most were found ready to do their duty."

The captain called for all hands on deck, and the men obeyed, led by the old boatswain William Kingsbury, David's friend. "Long shall I remember the cheering sound of his stentorian voice," Farragut said, "which resembled the roaring of a lion rather than that of a human being, when he told them, 'Damn your eyes! Put your best foot forward! There is one side of the ship left yet!"

Eventually the *Essex* made it round the Cape, though badly in need of repair. Finally, on March 15, the ship made port at Valparaiso, on the northwestern coast of Chile. A week later the *Essex* set out on a heroic cruise up the coast of Chile and Peru. Many American and British whaling ships used these waters, as well as Peruvian coast guard vessels, which were allied with the British. At one point the *Essex* captured a Peruvian ship and found the hold full of captured American whaling-ship sailors. The crew of the *Essex* welcomed them aboard, and many of these sailors signed on to join the *Essex*.

At another point two British whalers fired their guns at them. When the *Essex* pulled up close, the captain demanded that the whaling ships surrender to the United States. To their surprise, the men of the *Essex* heard the reply: "We are all Americans!" It seemed the crews of these boats were all American men who had been forced into British service.

In this cruise the *Essex* captured seven British whalers in all and recaptured one American ship, the *Barclay*. Following this capture there came an important event in David Farragut's life.

Captain Porter's task now was to escort some of the captured ships to safe harbor. Each captured ship was called a "prize," and each prize was operated by a "prize crew" from the *Essex*. The officer put in charge of the *Barclay* was Farragut. The 12-year-old was to command his own crew for a distance of 2,500 miles back to Valparaiso!

Despite Farragut's youth, his crew was happy to serve under him, for they had come to respect him. But the captain of the *Barclay*, "a violent-tempered old fellow," was not at all pleased to have a boy running his ship. He felt certain Farragut would get them lost at sea, or worse.

"When the day arrived for our separation from the squadron," Farragut wrote, "the captain was furious, and very plainly intimated to me that I would 'find myself off New Zealand in the morning.'" But the boy would not be bullied. "I considered that my day of trial had arrived," he wrote. He ordered the sails filled. At this the captain leaped to his feet and swore he would shoot anyone who touched a rope without his order. With that he disappeared below deck in search of his pistols.

Farragut quickly ordered men to fill the sails, which they did. The ship was now his; he had proved himself. For good measure, he informed the captain not to come on deck with his pistols unless he wanted to be thrown overboard. As Farragut wrote much later, "I felt no little pride in finding myself in command at twelve years of age."

After the prizes had been safely escorted to Valparaiso, there came a time of rest for the sailors. The *Essex* was now accompanied by a smaller warship, taken from the enemy. Captain Porter dubbed it the *Essex Junior*. The two ships reached the Galapagos Islands in the Pacific Ocean off the coast of Ecuador, an uninhabited group of islands that was home to a fantastic variety of exotic sea and plant life. Today the Galapagos are protected as a natural wonder. In 1813

David Farragut and his fellow crew members must have thought they were in paradise. Everything they could desire was there, fresh water and plentiful food. They found great numbers of terrapins (huge turtles) to eat. "The meat, cooked in almost any manner, is delicious," said Farragut.

He described the marvels they found when they arrived: "We found a spring about three miles from the beach. Birds were in great abundance, particularly doves, and we made a potpie of them, cooked the terrapin in his shell, and so made a feast. The prickly pear of the Galapagos grows very large, and the fruit, which we ate for dessert, has an excellent flavor. These were among the happiest days of my life."

From the Galapagos they made their way to the Marquesas, islands far out in the South Pacific. They stayed for six weeks in this tropical paradise. Farragut and the other young midshipmen became friends with the boys of the village. "From them we learned how to throw the spear and walk on stilts," he wrote.

Finally it was time to leave. First, however, came an unpleasant task. "We refitted the ship and smoked out the rats," Farragut wrote, "which had become so numerous as to endanger our safety, for they were actually cutting through the water-casks, and even into the skin of the ship."

On February 3, 1814, the *Essex* and the *Essex Junior* again reached the port of Valparaiso, Chile. Here Captain Porter made what some would call a tragic error. The port was considered neutral, meaning that both American and British ships could dock there. One night, two British ships—the *Phoebe* and the *Cherub*—came into port armed for battle. The crews of the *Essex* and *Essex Junior* prepared for the worst, though technically combat was not permitted in a neutral port.

The lead ship, the *Phoebe*, made straight for the American ships. It showed no signs of slowing down, so the sailors prepared to fire their cannons. Suddenly, Captain Porter held them back, when he realized that the British captain was James Hillyar, an old friend of his. It seemed as if Captain Hillyar was pulling his ship alongside the *Essex* to greet his friend.

Finally, the *Phoebe* found itself between the *Essex* and the *Essex Junior*. At this point Captain Hillyar realized the dangerous position he had put himself in. His ship was an easy target.

The American sailors were itching for battle. The powder-boys (called "powder monkeys") stood by the cannons with slow matches, ready to light the fuses. One of these boys thought he saw the crew of the *Phoebe* laughing at him. He moved his hand down to touch the fuse. At that moment a lieutenant on the ship flew at the boy and knocked him away.

"Had that gun been fired," Farragut later wrote, "I am convinced that the *Phoebe* would have been ours." But no guns were fired. Captain Porter allowed the *Phoebe* to move off to a safe dock.

For the next several days the enemy crews stayed together in the town. The officers even met and had drinks. When Hillyar and Porter sat down together, Hillyar gravely told his colleague that it was a mistake to let him get away. He, Hillyar, would not have done the same thing. And, he said, Captain Porter might live to regret it. Hillyar was right.

The British ships were now anchored outside the harbor. One day a terrible storm hit the coast. The *Essex* was damaged and lost its mooring cables. It began drifting toward the British ships. The crew scrambled to put up the sails in order to blow past the enemy. But just as they came close a great wind nearly capsized the ship. Technically the ships were still in neutral waters, but Hillyar had warned Porter that he would ignore that neutrality. The British frigates moved forward.

Everyone on board the *Essex* knew they were doomed. "I well remember the feelings of awe produced in me by the approach of the hostile ships," Farragut said later.

The enemy opened fire. Captain Porter tried every tactic he could think of to escape the attack. The *Essex*'s guns blasted away, but they were hopelessly outnumbered and outmaneuvered. Fire broke out on the ship several times. Smoke choked the sailors, cannonballs blasted into them, blood spattered the deck. The battle lasted two hours. At the end, out of 258 men on board the *Essex*, 58 were dead and 66 wounded.

The *Essex* was finally defeated at Valparaiso, Chile, by the *Cherub* and the *Phoebe*.

The remainder of the crew were taken aboard the British vessels. David Farragut, not yet 13, became a prisoner on the *Phoebe*. To his dismay, he did not act very grown up. "I was so mortified at our capture that I could not refrain from tears," he said.

He was taken below deck, where the sailors were cheering their victory and dividing up the spoils from the ship that had been David's home for nearly three years. Suddenly he heard a young British officer, not much older than he, calling out, "A prize! A prize! Ho, boys, a fine grunter, by Jove!"

David saw that the boy had captured the *Essex*'s pet pig, which the crew had named Murphy. He was suddenly furious, as if capturing the pig were as bad as capturing the ship and crew. He stared at the boy. "That belongs to me," he said.

"Ah, but you are a prisoner, and your pig, also!" the boy cried.

"*We* always respect private property," said David coldly.

The other boy looked over his prisoner, smiled, and offered to fight for it.

"Agreed!" cried David. He was angry, and he put all his anger into the fight. He beat the boy soundly.

Much later, remembering that fight, Farragut said, "So I took Master Murphy under my arm, feeling I had, in some degree, wiped out the disgrace of our defeat."

Good Feelings, Sort of

"What! To be driven from our village and hunting
grounds, and not even permitted to visit the
graves of our forefathers...?"

BLACK HAWK, CHIEF OF THE SAK AND FOX

On Christmas Eve 1814, the war came to an end. The British, though much more powerful, decided that it was too costly to continue fighting. The Duke of Wellington, the influential statesman and war hero, convinced his countrymen to sign a peace treaty. He knew the Americans would fight forever if they had to, even though there was no hope of victory.

In fact, the two sides kept fighting for a time even after the war was officially over. The peace treaty was signed in Belgium so it took time for the news to travel to the United States. One of the bloodiest battles of the war—the Battle of New Orleans—took place on January 8, 1815, two weeks after the leaders had agreed to peace. The Americans beat their opponents in that final battle. Their commanding officer, Andrew Jackson, was a man who would become extremely important in the years to come.

When the war was over, the young, vigorous nation exploded with activity. In the North, the new industries that had been forming slowly suddenly came alive. In Massachusetts, Francis Cabot Lowell invented a cotton mill that combined all the complicated steps needed to make cotton fabric. Now textiles were made in factories by machines instead of by hand. Before the war Robert Fulton had built one of the first commercial steamboats. Since then the technology had been perfected so that steamboats were chugging up and down the Hudson River in New York. Soon they would replace flatboats on the mighty Mississippi itself. The concept of organizing work into factories and turning out complex machines caught on quickly.

The country also grew at an incredible rate in the decades following the war. Louisiana, David Farragut's boyhood home, became a state in 1812. Between 1816 and 1822, five more states were admitted to the Union: Indiana, Illinois, Alabama, Mississippi, and Missouri.

Groups of Native Americans had inhabited the forests and plains of the western frontier for centuries. Now they watched as settlers moved in and cleared the land. Many such groups tried to live side by side with the newcomers. But the settlers were determined to take all the land for themselves, even if it meant slaughtering whole tribes.

One chief, Tecumseh of the Shawnee, spoke for many Native Americans when he said, "Our lives are in the hands of the Great Spirit. We are determined to defend our lands, and if it be his will, we wish to leave our bones upon them."

As a leader of Native Americans in the Ohio Valley, Tecumseh tried to stop the spread of white settlements. Tecumseh's dream was to form a great American Indian nation composed of many groups, just as the American nation was made up of different states. Tecumseh saw the American settlers as invaders. He supported the British during the War of 1812 and helped them capture Detroit. He was finally killed in battle in 1813.

Another chief, Black Hawk, of the Sac and Fox Indians, expressed his outrage at the settlers' invasions: "What! To be driven from our village and hunting grounds, and not even permitted to visit the graves of our forefathers...?"

The newcomers saw themselves as pioneers, starting settlements that would grow into towns and cities, and eventually into states. As the decades went by, one tribe after another lost its homeland.

Tecumseh, chief of the Shawnee, worked valiantly to unite Indian tribes into one great nation.

As the country grew, it prospered. The years after the war came to be known as "the Era of Good Feelings," though the good feelings certainly didn't apply to the Native Americans. The different regions prospered in different ways. In time people from the Northeast, the South, and the West came to feel pride in their own special characteristics.

The West became known as the land of opportunity. A man who was unhappy with his life could take his family to the endless stretches of land, stake out his share, and begin farming. As more and more people farmed the West, it soon became the most important region for livestock, wheat, and corn.

Since these animals and crops were supplied cheaply in the West, northern farms began to disappear, to be replaced by more factories and workshops. The Industrial Revolution developed and thrived most widely in the Northeast. Northern factories produced clocks, firearms, engines, and tools. Northerners were proud of their successful businesses, and of the fact that they lived in the most developed part of the country.

The South prospered as well. Most of its success, however, came from just one crop, cotton. The vast expanses of rich land in the South were perfect for growing cotton; people settled there in greater and greater numbers. At the same time, demand for cotton was at an all-time high. All over the United States people wanted cotton for clothing. Even more important, Europe was eager to buy all the cotton the South could produce.

As the world market for cotton increased, Southerners struggled to keep up with the demand. They moved steadily westward, deeper and deeper into unsettled lands. Eli Whitney's invention of the cotton gin, a machine that removed the seeds from the cotton, made some farms even more profitable. But it also increased the South's dependence on slaves. The small farms grew into large plantations. Southern farmers had long relied on slaves to work their fields. Now, as the demand for cotton grew, the numbers of black slaves increased. In the early days of the nation, before the War of 1812, there were far fewer slaves in the South. People had told one another that slavery was an evil institution that would one day die out.

But now things changed radically. Southern plantation owners wanted to continue making large profits, so they changed their thinking about slaves. They decided that slavery was necessary because it made the country rich. In the North and, to a lesser degree, the South, there were many people opposed to slavery. But the fact was that the entire nation now depended on the money from the sale of Southern cotton abroad. Many argued that the cotton plantations would be unprofitable if they used regular paid workers. Slavery, they said, had become an economic necessity.

Still, as the Era of Good Feelings went along, arguments over the slavery issue became more heated. The good feelings were not so good anymore. The most hotly debated question was what to do about slavery in the new states and territories of the West. Should slavery be outlawed in these lands as they became states?

There were fiery debates in the Congress. The interesting thing was that the two sides were not the Federalists and the Democratic-Republicans, which were the two political parties. Instead, it was Northern senators arguing with Southern senators. Finally in 1820 a plan, called the Missouri Compromise, was agreed upon. The Southern areas in the West (what used to be the Louisiana Purchase) would be slave states, while the Northern areas would be free. The dividing line would be the southern border of Missouri, which was latitude 36° 30'. Slavery would be legal south of this line. North of this latitude, slavery would be illegal, except in the territory of Missouri. Missouri was to be admitted as a slave state and Maine as a free state.

After Congress passed this series of measures, tempers cooled for a time. But there was still a great deal of grumbling. The compromise didn't completely satisfy the American people, and everybody knew it could only be a temporary solution. The United States hadn't solved its big problem—it had simply agreed not to think about it for a while longer.

A REVOLUTION ON THE SEAS

"I am being steamed to death."

JAMES PAULDING, NAVY SECRETARY, 1830S

avid Farragut was a busy seaman in the years following the War of 1812. But despite his achievements he did not rise through the ranks quickly. The U.S. Navy had too many lieutenants, commanders, and captains at that time, so midshipmen were not able to advance. And since David had been so young when he joined the navy it meant that he would have to wait even longer for a promotion.

One of his assignments following the war, in the spring of 1816, was on the *Washington*, a 74-gun warship. It was commanded by the stern Captain Creighton, who was a fanatic for order and cleanliness aboard ship. Creighton drove his men nearly crazy with his strict, to-the-letter insistence on discipline. Midshipman Farragut made up his mind that if he were ever given his own command, he would run his ship differently. When men are made to suffer week in and week out for no purpose, he realized, they begin to resent their commander. Instead of becoming tougher sailors, they slouch whenever they get the chance.

Soon after Farragut signed aboard, the *Washington* set sail for Europe. The government was now anxious to protect American interests abroad. Merchant ships were always in danger of being attacked by pirates from the coast of North Africa, which was called the Barbary Coast. President James Monroe therefore sent the *Washington* on an extensive cruise of Mediterranean waters.

The *Washington* made stops in many cities on the Mediterranean, including Naples, Messina, and Malaga. Midshipman Farragut found the whole voyage a great adventure. He looked forward to each new stop. It was a chance to broaden his horizons, and also a chance to get away from the harsh life aboard the *Washington*.

One very good result of serving on the *Washington* was that Farragut became friends with the chaplain, Charles Folsom. It was common in those days for a ship's chaplain to give reading and writing lessons to the midshipmen. For many young seamen this was the only schooling they ever received. Folsom saw at once that Farragut was a bright, eager young man who soaked up knowledge.

For his part, David was deeply grateful for the attention the older man gave him. For all practical purposes, he had no family. It had been years since he left his home in New Orleans. He had seen none of his family since. Although he remained in close touch with Captain Porter, they were now assigned to different ships.

Then, in the summer of 1817, David got word from Louisiana that his father had died. Now he felt really alone. Mr. Folsom comforted David, listening to him talk about his father. David now felt closer to Chaplain Folsom than ever.

Later that year Folsom was appointed the American consul (diplomat) in the United States office in the Barbary Coast city of Tunis, today the capital of Tunisia. David was heartbroken at the news that his friend would leave him. Just as quickly, his spirits soared. Mr. Folsom got permission from the commander-in-chief to bring David with him to Tunis.

David spent the next year in this exotic city on the Mediterranean. He studied the ruins of the ancient city of Carthage, upon which Tunis was built. He visited the bazaars of the old city and explored its twisting alleyways. And when there was time, Folsom taught him English literature, French, Italian, and mathematics. David turned out to have a natural talent for languages.

At the end of the year, however, David was called back to service, this time aboard the *Franklin*, the flagship of a squadron of ships. He spent most of 1819 cruising the Mediterranean, chasing pirates with the squadron. Then, in the fall, when they were stationed off Gilbraltar, word came that one of the squadron's brigs, a two-masted, square-rigged ship, the *Shark*, needed a lieutenant. Midshipman Farragut was appointed acting lieutenant. It was a big promotion for David, who was now only 18 years old.

It would be several years before Farragut received another promotion. But this one was very important to him. As he later said, "It caused me to feel that I was now associated with men, on an equality, and must act with more circumspection."

In later life, Farragut thought he was very lucky that he had been given command at such a young age. "I consider it a great advantage to obtain command young," he said, "having observed, as a general rule, that persons who come into authority late in life shrink from responsibility, and often break down under its weight."

Lieutenant Farragut did not break down. For one year he served as second officer aboard the *Shark*. In fact, he often performed the captain's duties, saying, "[I]n truth I was really commander of the vessel."

In 1820, Farragut returned to the United States. It was a strange homecoming. He had no real family, no friends except for a few fellow officers. He settled where his ship docked, in Norfolk, Virginia. There he met a young woman named Susan Marchant. They decided to marry as soon as they could. But they would have to wait, for in May 1822, Lt. Farragut was again ordered to sea. This time he would sail the Caribbean.

David was sorry to leave his fiancée, but eager to serve under his new commander. He was assigned to a special pirate-chasing squadron headed by his guardian, Commodore David Porter. From Puerto Rico to Haiti and from Haiti to Cuba the brave squadron pursued some of the most dreaded pirates in the West Indies. It was a busy time. "I never owned a bed during my two years and a half in the West Indies," he said later, "but lay down to rest wherever I found the most comfortable berth."

All his hard work paid off. The squadron succeeded, for the most part, in ridding the Caribbean of piracy. Beaten at sea, the criminals took to land, where the various Spanish governments that ruled the islands eventually hunted them down.

Upon his return to Norfolk, Farragut wasted no time. He and Susan were married on September 2, 1824. After the wedding they traveled to Washington to visit Commodore Porter, who was ill with an attack of yellow fever. Then the Farraguts returned to Norfolk to set up housekeeping.

Farragut's pay was only $25 a month, and in addition to supporting his wife he regularly sent money to his two sisters, Nancy and Elizabeth, still living with their foster families in Louisiana. This meant that the newly married couple had to work hard and save to make ends meet.

Farragut's career advanced steadily over the next several years. On January 13, 1825 he was appointed lieutenant, and his pay was increased to $40 per month. He made two trips to South America, putting in at ports in Argentina and Brazil. In 1833 he was made first lieutenant of the man-of-war *Natchez* and sent to Charleston, South Carolina. President Andrew Jackson had ordered troops to deal with uprisings there after South Carolina had "nullified," or refused to honor, the national tax laws.

In 1838, Farragut commanded the sloop-of-war *Erie*, which was ordered to the east coast of Mexico. France was now at war with Mexico, and Farragut's duty was to protect American interests. He observed the attack on Veracruz by the French admiral Baudin. He noted carefully how certain shells were useless against the forts while others blasted holes in the walls. Later Farragut would become a national hero for his capture of New Orleans in the Civil War. This knowledge of bombardment from the sea would be of great importance then.

As David Farragut's career advanced, so did the United States Navy. In the decades following the War of 1812, a quiet revolution in sea power was taking place. Throughout history there had been only two ways to move a boat through the open seas: with manpower, using oars, or with wind power, using sails. But with the arrival of the steam engine, nothing would be the same again.

By the 1820s steamboats were cruising along most of the nation's major rivers, carrying passengers and supplies between distant ports. Oddly enough, the navy was slow to make the change to steam power. Its officials believed there were too many problems with steamships to make them workable in military service. Some even thought the new engines were only a passing fad, and that after a time sails would once again be the usual way to power a boat.

The secretary of the navy, James Paulding, was one of the most severe critics of steamboats. In fact, Paulding had several good reasons for not wanting to rely on them. Compared with later technology, the first engines were very crude. They often broke down, and they could not travel even a hundred miles without needing to be refueled.

Steadily, other leaders in the navy and government pressed Paulding to make the change to steam power. The pressure to change became so intense that Paulding once complained, "I am being steamed to death."

But the change finally came. In 1839 the nation's first two steam-powered warships—the *Mississippi* and the *Missouri*—put to sea. The revolution in sea power was finally underway. But the new crafts were not strictly steamships. For several decades all ships would have sails as well, because no one completely trusted the newfangled engines.

The navy in which David Farragut grew to manhood was changing in some ways. In other ways, it was very old-fashioned. The life of a seaman had always been harsh, and it was no different in Farragut's day. In fact, in the years following the War of 1812, conditions for the average sailor worsened. There was always a shortage of food aboard ship, the pay was low, there were few doctors, and fewer medicines available. And worst of all was the punishment that was given to disobedient or lazy sailors.

The dreaded cat-o-nine-tails whip was still used for flogging. Officers routinely flogged, or whipped, their sailors for the smallest infractions. The worst punishment was keelhauling, dragging a sailor underwater, completely underneath the boat, the whole distance along the keel, or bottom spine.

Such types of cruel punishment were slow to disappear from the navy, despite modernization in other areas. One former sailor, however, took it upon himself to make the country aware of the barbarous conditions under which so many young sailors lived. His name was Herman Melville. He had served aboard the frigate *United States* in 1843–44, as well as on several whaling ships. Afterward he began writing novels of sea life, including his masterpiece *Moby-Dick*, published in 1851. Through Melville's books the public learned of the terrible conditions that existed on naval ships. Gradually, as the decades wore on, regulations were passed forbidding certain kinds of punishment, such as keelhauling and flogging. Flogging had been so commonplace that in Melville's year aboard the *United States*, he reported that crewmen were beaten more than 160 times. The new regulations also standardized pay, shore leave, and other benefits sailors were to receive.

In the years between the War of 1812 and the Civil War, the U.S. Navy had several important missions. One was to stop pirates from attacking American vessels. Another was to expand trade with other nations. In 1852 President Millard Fillmore decided that the United States should trade not only with European nations, but with the countries of the Pacific as well. So he ordered the navy to open up trade with Japan.

It may seem odd that a president relied on the military to establish trade. But the fact was that Japan was not interested in dealing with outsiders. The Japanese had been isolated from the outside world for centuries...and they liked it that way.

But if the president wanted to open up trade, the navy was determined to open up trade. Commodore Matthew Perry enthusiastically took on the job of forcing the Japanese into trading with

Following Commodore Perry's militant entry into Japan, a Japanese delegation arrived in the United States.

the United States. In 1853 Perry's four warships chugged into Uraga Harbor, on the main Japanese island of Honshu. Their cannons were pointed at the palace. Within a short time Perry forced the shogun, the military ruler of Japan, to agree to sell fuel and supplies to passing American ships. He also got approval for a permanent United States representative to be based in the Japanese city of Shimoda. He was later assured by the Japanese that they would deal humanely with shipwrecked sailors.

Many people would consider this kind of "gunboat diplomacy" an abuse of our naval power. But the United States government had decided it would establish ties by any means. The nation had grown strong and, fair or not, was showing its muscle.

A New Kind of Nation

"Take possession first and negotiate afterwards.
That is precisely what President Polk has done."
STEPHEN DOUGLAS, ON THE MEXICAN WAR

In January 1839, Lt. David Farragut, now 38 years old, asked for a leave of absence from his ship, which was stationed in Florida. He rushed to his home in Norfolk. There he found Susan, his wife, gravely ill with neuralgia, a painful nerve disease. When he learned how serious her condition was, he canceled plans to return to sea. For almost two years he was constantly at her side, talking with her, doing whatever he could to make her comfortable. In December of 1840, Susan Farragut died.

David had been so diligent and loving in caring for his wife that one of the women of the town later remarked, "When Captain Farragut dies, he should have a monument reaching to the skies, made by every wife in the city contributing a stone."

After his wife's death, Farragut was heartbroken. Not surprisingly, the only possible cure he could think of for the sorrow he felt was the sea. He requested assignment, and was ordered to report to the ship *Delaware*, which was leaving Norfolk for Brazil at the head of a squadron.

The squadron had not been in Brazil very long when the commander of one of the smaller ships became ill. He was Henry

Ogden, who had served as midshipman with Farragut on the *Essex*. With Ogden gone, a replacement was needed. Lt. David Farragut was chosen. At last, after more than 30 years in the navy, he was promoted to the rank of commander. He was 40 years old.

In 1846, another important change came for Farragut and for the entire nation. In the decades prior to the Civil War the United States began to realize that it was a powerful nation. It had expanded its territory enormously, and wanted to keep expanding. As settlers continued moving westward beyond the Mississippi River, they were entering land that did not belong to the United States.

Many keen-eyed observers could see the trouble coming. A Frenchman named Alexis de Tocqueville visited the United States in 1831. He wrote: "The inhabitants of the United States are perpetually migrating to Texas.... The province of Texas is still part of the Mexican dominions, but it will soon contain no Mexicans." Settlers in Texas won their independence from Mexico in 1836, and in 1845 the United States declared Texas a part of the nation.

The area that now makes up the states of California, Utah, and Nevada, as well as parts of Arizona, New Mexico, Wyoming, and Colorado, was also owned by Mexico. But more and more Americans were settling there. The Mexican government was not pleased. Something was bound to happen.

In 1845, President James K. Polk entered office determined to add these western lands to the United States. The country was swept up in expansion fever. One Baltimore newspaper said, "The process by which Texas was acquired may be repeated over and over again."

Mexico, meanwhile, was still angry over the loss of Texas. But the Mexican government was not able to do anything about it because it had only just won its own independence from Spain in 1821, and since that time it had suffered a series of bloody revolutions. American property was destroyed in these revolutions, and many American settlers were killed. This added more tension to relations between the United States and her southern neighbor.

Finally, in 1846, President Polk decided it was time for the western lands to become an official part of the United States. He ordered troops, under General Zachary Taylor, to the Rio Grande. The United States claimed that this river was the border between the two countries. Mexico, however, claimed that a river farther north was the border. The Mexicans sent troops into this disputed area to guard against invasion.

On April 23, 1846, gunfire sounded as the two armies clashed. Sixteen American soldiers were killed. President Polk now had an excuse for asking Congress to declare war. Some members of Congress questioned whether the United States had good reason for going to war. Some politicians worried that an American victory would mean that more slave states such as Texas would become part of the nation. One such congressman was young Abraham Lincoln, of Illinois. Despite the protests of these representatives, war was declared.

When war broke out, Farragut was stationed at the navy yard in Norfolk. His eyes lit up when he heard the news. This meant a chance to go into action. He immediately dashed off a letter to the Navy Department asking for an assignment. He listed his impressive record of service, in case the administrators neglected to consult his file. He added that he spoke Spanish, which might come in very handy.

When his letter was not answered, Farragut wrote another. This time he offered advice. San Juan de Ulua was a small island in the Gulf of Mexico off the east coast of Mexico. A castle stood there guarding the entrance to the harbor of the port city of Veracruz. Farragut believed this stronghold could be taken by a concerted naval bombardment. He had been to Veracruz in 1838, during one of his voyages, so he was familiar with the area. He outlined his battle plan.

The Navy Department finally answered Farragut's requests, giving him command of the warship *Saratoga* in February 1847. He set off at once for Veracruz. In his mind he could picture the glorious victory that lay ahead. It would bring honor to him, and also to the navy, which needed some attention in Washington if it was to keep pace with the army in prestige and resources.

But when the *Saratoga* came into Veracruz harbor, Farragut's dreams vanished. The castle had already been taken by the United States Army. It might seem strange that Farragut should be disappointed that the Americans had won a major victory, as if the U.S. Navy and U.S. Army were at war with one another.

It was not quite that bad, but many naval officers, including David Farragut, were concerned that the army was getting more attention and money than the navy. These officers felt that the navy was not being modernized as it should be, and that the navy officials in Washington were doing a poor job of managing things. Some of them jokingly called the navy's Bureau of Construction, Equipment, and Repair the "Bureau of Destruction and Despair."

Farragut was hoping that a big naval victory in the Mexican War would enhance the navy's image. But it did not happen. Farragut did not get another chance to fight. There was an outbreak of yellow fever on the *Saratoga*, with 100 of the 150 men aboard, including Farragut, getting the disease. His case was so severe that for a time his doctor believed he would die. At the end of the war, Farragut was a sad, weakened man.

The Mexican War lasted two years, from 1846 to 1848. By the end, all the territory from Texas to California was in American hands. A victory had been won. Most Americans were happy. It seemed that a new day was dawning.

The nation had indeed matured in its 75 years of history. Back in the days following the Revolutionary War, many Europeans had believed the struggling country would not be able to govern itself. Its economy would collapse, they said. The government would not be able to lead. European thinkers were interested in the "experiment" that the Americans were trying. It was a new form of government called a democracy, based on ideas of individual rights, in which the people ruled either directly or indirectly through elected officials. The idea of democracy was born in Greece thousands of years before. But nobody really believed it could work. After all, they asked themselves, how could the people govern themselves? The masses of people were poor, uneducated farmers. They knew nothing about government.

But now, 75 years later, the American experiment seemed to be working. The new country was still growing in size and strength. It had fought wars, gained new territory, and was supplying enormous quantities of goods to European markets. Now Europeans began coming to the United States themselves. Waves of poor immigrants—mostly from Germany and Ireland—arrived on the shores of the United States, hoping to start a new life. The newcomers found jobs in the factories and sweatshops of the East. They were willing to work for very low wages. Factories flourished with such cheap labor. And the country grew wealthier by the day.

But as prosperity grew, so did problems. In the old days the nation had really been just a loose group of cities, townships, and counties. Most things were done locally. Ordinary people did not pay much attention to the federal government, or to things outside their region. Washington, D.C., seemed as far away as the moon.

As the 19th century wore on, however, change came rapidly. Railroads stretched across the land, bringing goods and people from far away into small communities. As large factories developed, people began to rely on products from other places instead of making their own or buying locally. Stores in New England now sold wheat grown in the Midwest. General stores on the western frontier stocked shoes, hats, and gloves produced in eastern factories. In this way, hundreds of tiny communities were brought closer together.

This led to problems. People began to resent outsiders. The new immigrants were laughed at and forced to live under the poorest conditions. The North resented the South, which controlled the cotton industry. The South resented the North, which controlled the factories. These economic differences brought arguments on other issues, including states' rights in the federal Union. Southern states believed they had the right to break away, or secede, from the Union if they felt it was necessary. Northern states argued that the Union was indivisible, that no state could simply decide to break away.

The most explosive problem of all, however, was slavery. Politicians had tried to ignore it for a long time. Now they could ignore it no longer. During the 1850s Congress again debated the issue of slavery in the new territories. Different compromises were tried, then fell apart. In 1858, a little-known Illinois congressman named Abraham Lincoln held a series of debates with his opponent, Stephen Douglas. Lincoln announced to the audience, "This government cannot endure permanently half *slave* and half *free*."

The country was deeply divided. Many now believed war was just around the corner. Serious thinkers had long recognized that the slavery issue was liable to tear the nation apart. As early as 1835—26 years before the Civil War would break out—the visiting Frenchman Alexis de Tocqueville wrote:

"If ever America undergoes great revolutions, they will be brought about by the presence of the black race on the soil of the United States—that is to say, they will owe their origin, not to the equality, but to the inequality, of conditions."

The visitor from abroad, de Tocqueville, had spied the flaw in the American democracy. The equality that the Constitution promised was still only a fiction. The fiction had gone on long enough. War was about to test the strength of the country's founding principles.

A TALE OF TWO NAVIES

"What about this new vessel, the *Monitor*?"
EDWIN STANTON, UNION SECRETARY OF WAR

he general store in Norfolk, Virginia, was packed tight on April 18, 1861. People filled the aisles, crowded around the counter, spilled out onto the street. Excitement crackled through the place like electricity. The news had just reached them that the Virginia state convention had voted to join other Southern states and secede from the Union.

Captain David Farragut hurried to the store as soon as he could. It was a place to meet local men and discuss events. Farragut was now a regular resident of Norfolk, where he had again been stationed. It was here that he met Virginia Loyall, the daughter of one of Norfolk's leading citizens, and they married on December 26, 1843. Shortly afterward, Farragut was appointed executive officer aboard the ship of the line *Pennsylvania*. His high rank meant that he would have quarters provided for himself and his wife, so the new Mrs. Farragut lived aboard ship. On October 12, 1844, she gave birth to a son, Loyall, named after her family.

Over the following years, the Farraguts became model citizens of Norfolk. Mrs. Farragut attended civic functions, and everyone was proud to have Commander Farragut as a neighbor. In 1847 Farragut left for service in the Mexican War, and in 1854, he traveled to California to help establish a navy yard in San Francisco. His duties kept him busy, and his wife and son had a good life in Norfolk.

Then, in November 1860, Abraham Lincoln was elected president. Most Southerners had supported the Democratic candidate John Breckinridge, who was pro-slavery. Only three days after the election, South Carolina called together a "secession convention." The next month South Carolina became the first state to formally leave the Union. Others quickly followed, and in February 1861 representatives gathered in Montgomery, Alabama, to form a new government. They adopted a constitution and elected Jefferson Davis, formerly a United States senator from Mississippi, president of this newly formed association of states called the Confederacy.

Farragut had been hoping that Virginia would remain neutral and avoid siding with the other states of the South. The war, which would tear apart families and towns, was tearing him in two directions as well. He had been born and raised in the South. But most of his adult life had been spent at sea, in the service of his country. So he also had deep feelings for the United States as a nation.

In the local tavern were many of his fellow officers, friends and acquaintances. He entered hoping to discuss the matter intelligently with them. But he saw at once that with the vote to secede, everything had changed. His comrades, officers in the U.S. Navy, now talked as though the United States were their bitterest enemy.

Besides the vote to secede, there was one other topic that excited the crowd. A week before, on April 12, Confederate soldiers had attacked Fort Sumter, a U.S. Army stronghold at the entrance to Charleston harbor, in South Carolina. The small group of soldiers stationed there was no match for the Southern troops massed around it. The fort fell.

With this act, the Civil War began. All of Norfolk was buzzing with talk of the battle. White Southerners, it seemed, felt more allegiance to the South than to the nation.

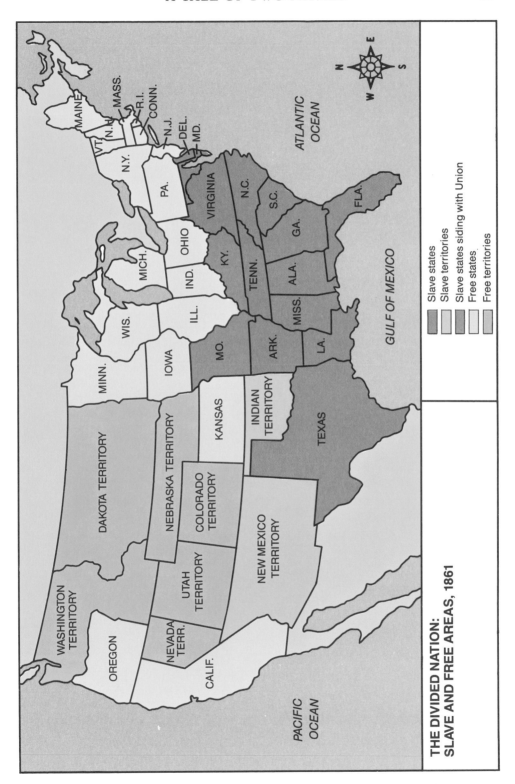

**THE DIVIDED NATION:
SLAVE AND FREE AREAS, 1861**

Slave states
Slave territories
Slave states siding with Union
Free states
Free territories

Nevertheless, Farragut talked to his friends with his usual bluntness. He expressed his opinion that the South Carolinians were wrong to attack an American fort. President Lincoln had called for 75,000 men to volunteer to defend the Republic. Farragut told the assembly he believed the president had no other choice.

At this the tavern erupted. One man shouted that anyone with such feelings should not be living in Norfolk. Others cheered.

Farragut scanned the crowd, a frown on his face. "Very well," he said in low but firm tones. "I can live somewhere else." He turned on his heel and walked out of the tavern. Then, a thought crossing his mind, he looked inside and said grimly, "Mind what I tell you: You fellows will catch the devil before you get through with this business."

So the decision was made. He had delayed as long as possible, but now that he had made up his mind he lost no time. He went back home and told his wife that he would be leaving to go north. He then pointed out to her that if she accompanied him, she would be separated from her family and friends, possibly for many years. The decision was hers. Mrs. Farragut said she would go with him.

That very evening the family boarded a steamer bound for Baltimore. Eventually they reached New York, where they found a home. From now on David Farragut, son of the South, would be a Northerner and fight to preserve the Union.

Captain Farragut would soon see action, for the Union navy was to play a crucial role in the Civil War.

At first most of the government leaders in Washington gave little thought to the navy. Everyone thought the war would be brief. When President Lincoln called for recruits, it was only for 90 days. By that time, he hoped, the uprising in the South would be settled.

But Lincoln's commanding general, Winfield Scott, saw things differently. Scott had been a hero in the Mexican War. Now he was old, overweight, and in such poor health he could hardly get up from his desk without help. But he was still in command, and he saw the situation more clearly than anyone else.

Scott knew that the South would not be so easy to put down. True, the North had many advantages. Almost all of the country's

Virginia Farragut was a Southerner, but she followed her husband north at the onset of war.

factories were in the North, so that it could produce the goods it needed. It had a much larger population—20 million, as opposed to only 9 million in the South. Most of the hundreds of miles of railroad tracks that had been laid down over the past few decades were in the North. This would mean troops and supplies could be transported quickly. To many people, the South seemed hopelessly backward.

But the South had several big advantages. For one thing, as Scott knew, it is always easier to fight defensively than offensively. The defending army can dig trenches and pick off enemy soldiers as they attack. In order to make the sides equal, Scott knew, the North would need all its extra manpower.

Also, most of the war would be fought in the South. This meant that the "rebels" would have the advantage of knowing the terrain and the roads. They would be able to rely on the local people for food, supplies, and aid, as well.

So Scott believed the war would drag on for a long time. Other Union generals favored a quick strike at Richmond, Virginia, the capital city of the Confederacy. This, they felt, would bring the war to an end quickly. "On to Richmond!" was their cry. But Scott had a very different plan. He proposed that the Union navy blockade the Southern coast, so that the Confederacy could not get supplies from Europe. Then, he added, the Mississippi River should be controlled by the North. In this way the South would be cut off from the western states.

At first the Union high command rejected Scott's plan, which was named the Anaconda Plan, after the snake that kills its victim by squeezing them to death. In time, however, President Lincoln came to see that the war would drag on. He then turned to the Anaconda Plan.

As far as David Farragut was concerned, the Union had to take advantage of one other thing in its favor: its navy. In the decade after the Mexican War the government had finally come to realize the importance of a modern, well-equipped navy. The new secretary of the navy, Gideon Welles, had navy yards all over the country at his disposal, ready to build ships. The department had become more efficient. Officers who were too old or feeble to serve were retired, and younger men took their places.

The next step was, of course, to build the necessary ships. At the start of the war the North had only 24 good warships. When President Lincoln realized the conflict might drag on for a long time, he ordered construction to begin. In New York, Boston,

Washington, Philadelphia, and many other cities, navy yards went to work. Engineers laid out their plans, hammers rang out, laborers worked furiously.

The Civil War came at a crucial time in the history of naval technology. Two revolutions were going on while the country fought: the steam revolution and the "ironclad" revolution. Of course, steamers had been around for several decades, but they had not yet completely replaced sailing vessels. For now most ships were being built with both steam engines and sails. And as for iron-shielding, it was a new technology. Only two other countries in the world possessed ships covered with iron. They were England and France, and each country had only one such ship.

So while the North and South scrambled for ships, they were also scrambling to get ahead in the latest technology. Both sides experimented with iron ships. There were also many other unusual vessels created by the imaginative engineers of both sides. In 1863 Horace Hunley, a Southerner, unveiled a long, skinny contraption that had sailors scratching their heads. He called it a submarine. Hunley had experimented with several other submarines, but this one, named the C.S.S. *Hunley*, was his pride and joy.

The *Hunley* sank three times in test runs and killed 20 crewmen. But the inventor made improvements and insisted his ship would be ready for battle. Hunley himself was aboard, along with a crew of seven men, during its first battle in Charleston harbor. In battle the *Hunley* demonstrated her amazing ability to dive underwater and rise to the surface again. But after one of the dives the strange ship did not come back up. Hunley and his crew died on the floor of the harbor.

Some time later the Southern navy dragged the ship back to the surface and repaired it. It fought one more battle, in which it demonstrated that a submarine had potential military use. It sank the Union ship *Housatonic*, but unfortunately the *Hunley* sank, too—this time, for good.

The most famous of all battles involving the "high technology" of the Civil War navies occurred on March 9, 1862. On that day two of the strangest warships ever to put to sea met in combat.

The C.S.S. *Hunley* was one of the oddest, and most ill-fated, crafts used in the Civil War.

When the Civil War began, the South took control of the Union navy yard in Norfolk. Before the Union sailors retreated they scuttled one of their prize ships, the *Merrimack*. Scuttling means destroying your own vessel so that the invading enemy cannot use it. Eventually the Southerners raised the *Merrimack*, which was one of the best steamers in the navy, and refurbished it. They rebuilt it completely, constructing walls that slanted upwards out of the water. These they covered with a four-inch-thick iron plating, with holes in it for 10 cannons. When they were done, their creation looked like a kind of long, floating tank. They renamed it the C.S.S. *Virginia* (although Northerners still called it the *Merrimack*).

The Union Navy panicked when they found out about the ironclad vessel. They feared such a ship because no known artillery shell could pierce it. The ironclads were slow and awkward, but nearly indestructible. On March 8, 1862, the *Virginia* chugged boldly into the coastal waters, maneuvered slowly into position, and promptly sank two of the Union navy's best warships.

Fortunately for the North, its own ironclad, the *Monitor*, designed by the Swedish-American engineer John Ericsson, had just been completed. It was a strange-looking beast, too. Whereas the *Virginia*'s walls rose out of the water like a metal castle, the *Monitor* did not seem to have any walls at all. In the water it looked like a wide, flat platform of iron in the middle of which rose the rounded turret housing the guns.

The day after the *Virginia* made its dramatic debut, the two ships met in one of the oddest and most famous battles of the Civil War. All day long the vessels pounded one another with shells. The ironsides were a mass of dents by the end, but both ships survived. In the end the *Virginia* retreated. The battle was a major victory, but not for the North or South. The winner was military technology. A new era in naval ships was ushered in with the clash of the *Monitor* and *Virginia*.

THE BLOCKADE STRATEGY

"...the true test of the efficiency of the blockade
will be found in its results."
WILLIAM H. SEWARD, UNION SECRETARY OF STATE

In April 1861, shortly after the Confederacy bombarded Fort Sumter and signaled the beginning of the war, President Lincoln made an expensive and difficult political move. He issued a proclamation stating that the Union would "blockade" the Southern states, closing off their trade with Europe. He hoped this would force the South to surrender quickly.

As soon as the proclamation was made public European countries took notice. The word "blockade" is used only when referring to a foreign power. By using it, Lincoln had admitted that the South was no longer a part of the country. The Europeans now saw the South as a separate nation. They began to ask themselves whether they should favor one side or the other.

The other problem with Lincoln's proclamation was that the North simply did not have enough ships to blockade the Southern coast. There were only a few dozen ships in the navy, and some of them needed repairs. How could they guard 3,000 miles of coastline?

Secretary of the Navy Gideon Welles answered this question by ordering every shipyard in the North to work. He also signed contracts with Northern machine factories for engines and ship parts. One of the nation's fastest military buildups was now in progress. Although in the beginning the navy had only about 24 usable vessels, by the end of the war the Union possessed 900 seaworthy ships.

At first, the North had to use whatever was available. The navy commissioned all sorts of vessels for blockade duty. Whaling ships, small fishing boats, flatboats—just about anything that would float was outfitted with guns and sent South to patrol the coast. The mission of every captain was to stop merchant vessels loaded with goods from entering or exiting Southern harbors.

Union ships dotted the horizon off Southern ports. The blockade choked off supplies.

Surprisingly enough, the ragtag blockade worked. The South fought valiantly, but the North's naval blockade slowly strangled the enemy, Anaconda fashion. In the end, the blockade was as much responsible for the victory of the North as any other action of the war.

The North and South had very different ideas about how to use their naval power in the Civil War. This was because the two sides were in such different situations. The North had factories and shipyards. The South had few, and was in the impossible situation of trying to wage war at sea with virtually no ships.

Of course, this could not be done. The South had to get ships. In charge of this task was the South's secretary of the navy, a shrewd, imaginative man named Stephen Russell Mallory. Mallory was wise enough to see advantages in the South's position. It was true that the North had many ships in its navy. But Mallory also knew that technology was changing rapidly, and most of those ships were now outdated. A small number of modern vessels could help the South tremendously.

One of the first things Mallory did was to hire James Bulloch as his assistant. Bulloch was an experienced diplomat with a sharp mind who was good at tackling legal problems. How could such a man help build ships? He could not. Bulloch and Mallory decided at once that the South would have to buy ships. They turned to Europe.

Immediately, they faced a major problem. The European countries were neutral in the war, supporting neither side. Countries like England and France still traded with both the North and the South, though the blockade made it difficult to buy cotton from the South. Europe would not recognize the South as a nation in its own right until the war turned in its favor.

On the other hand, many European leaders quietly supported the South. The United States was a brash newcomer to the family of nations. In the few decades the nation had been in existence, it had grown larger than any European nation. It had also become amazingly prosperous. It had mile after mile of rich lands and hard-working people to farm them. Its Eastern factories were competing with Europe's. It also had a new democratic form of government that freed the people to grow in every way, especially financially.

Many European nations were not especially happy to see such success. They would have liked nothing better than for the bold young country to be split into two. Two weak nations would be more dependent on Europe, and easier to handle.

Stephen Mallory, Confederate Secretary of the Navy, was one of the most imaginative men in the war.

Still, James Bulloch had to use all of his diplomatic skill to arrange for English companies to build Confederate ships. English law stated that this would be a violation of its laws of neutrality. But Bulloch cleverly got around the law by having the British build regular merchant vessels. Later, after delivery, they could be outfitted with guns and iron plating.

Secretary Mallory was also shrewd. He realized that many of the Union's warships could not be used against the South. These ships had been designed for battle on the high seas, against enemies in Europe or South America. The navy's engineers and designers had never imagined the need to build vessels to fight their own countrymen. But many of the rivers in the South were winding and narrow, and the harbors were shallow. The big, graceful Union frigates would be useless in the South.

Mallory built his own ships with these facts in mind. They would be strong and swift, yet small enough to turn and move in the tight harbors and rivers. They were also outfitted with battering rams for smashing into enemy ships.

The Laird ram, seen on the Confederate ironclad *Stonewall*, could devastate wooden-hulled ships.

Mallory constructed these vessels to battle the blockading ships. He also built a small fleet of lightning-fast boats whose mission was to swoop down on enemy merchant ships. The daredevil crews of these raiders managed to throw the North's shipping into panic and confusion. For a time things looked up for the Confederacy. Its navy was in good hands and performing well against impossible odds.

9

FARRAGUT GETS THE CALL

"I am to have a flag in the Gulf, and the rest depends upon myself."

DAVID FARRAGUT, ON BEING MADE FLAG OFFICER

One afternoon in November 1861, five men in Washington, D.C., sat grimly around a table. Their task was to decide the course of the Civil War. At the head of the table, his face sad and stony, was President Abraham Lincoln. The issue being discussed was control of the Gulf of Mexico and the Mississippi River. Everyone agreed that the Union had to achieve this, but the question was how.

The North was using the same tactic that Great Britain had used in the War of 1812: blockading the enemy's ports. This meant putting a ring of warships around the South, from the Atlantic Coast through the Gulf of Mexico and up the Mississippi River.

In the Atlantic things had gone well. The blockade was helped by the capture of several harbors and forts along the coast. The ships of Flag Officer Louis Goldsborough and the army of Brigadier General Ambrose Burnside joined forces to pound away at Fort Macon, North Carolina. The fort fell. With it, the Union now controlled much of the North Carolina coast.

In South Carolina, another expedition bombarded Fort Beauregard and Fort Walker until the Confederate troops were forced to surrender. Port Royal, South Carolina, a vital naval base on the coast, fell to Union control. The Union's blockading vessels could now use Port Royal as their base.

The key to successfully blockading the Gulf of Mexico and the Mississippi River was New Orleans, the largest city in the Confederacy. Sitting just north of the Mississippi delta, where the river flowed into the Gulf, the city was crucial to Southern shipping. Without it, the South would be cut off from the world.

The Confederate leaders were concerned about protecting New Orleans. They put as much protection as they could manage to find along the river just north of the city. Any invasion, they knew, would come from the north because the mouth of the Mississippi to the south was full of settled mud so that no ships could get through.

This was just what Gustavus Fox believed the Southerners would be thinking. Fox was the assistant secretary of the navy. His task at the meeting was to urge President Lincoln to strike New Orleans from the south, taking the city by surprise.

Lincoln listened quietly. He knew little about naval matters, and he did not like the sound of the plan. It seemed extremely risky. He turned to Gideon Welles, his bushy-whiskered secretary of the navy. What was his opinion?

Welles nodded gravely. It was risky, but not as harebrained as a non-navy man might think. Such things had been done before. He urged the president to give the navy a chance.

Lincoln turned next to General George McClellan, who had recently been named commander of the Army of the Potomac, the army protecting Washington, and the centerpiece of the Union forces, replacing General Scott. McClellan, a stocky, excitable young general, expressed concern. He liked the boldness of the plan but, being an army man, did not know how capable the navy was of pulling it off. And besides, he wondered, who would lead the expedition? Did the navy have an officer capable of carrying out such a daring mission?

Here the fifth man at the table spoke up. He was Commander David Dixon Porter, one of the navy's finest officers. As the son of old Captain David Porter, hero of the War of 1812, he knew one man who would be perfect for the job: David Farragut, Captain Porter's adopted son and apprentice.

Eyebrows shot up. Everyone knew of Farragut's long service and his reputation for efficiency, but there were problems. First, could he be trusted? One of the biggest problems for the North in the early days of the war was Southern spies and defectors. Farragut was a son of the South. Perhaps he was waiting for just such a moment to show his true feelings for his homeland.

Porter knew his step-brother well, though the two had never lived in the same house together. Porter had been born while young David Farragut was a crewman aboard the *Essex*. Still, he had no doubts about David Farragut's loyalty to the United States and its navy. So the bushy-bearded commander immediately put to rest any fears of disloyalty.

The other problem with selecting Farragut was his age. He was 60 years old now. Could he handle such a difficult task?

Here again, Porter silenced the critics. Farragut, he told them, celebrated every birthday by turning a handspring. Any 60-year-old man who could do that was fit for service. What is more, when the mood struck him, the spry naval officer had been known to hold his left foot with his right hand, then jump back and forth over his leg!

Eventually President Lincoln was won over to the plan and to selecting Farragut as flag officer of the fleet, responsible for leading the expedition. As for David Farragut, when he met with Gustavus Fox and learned that he was to be given command of what was possibly the most important naval mission in the war, he burst with enthusiasm. Farragut had been given a dull desk job in Washington because his superiors were still uncertain about his loyalty, and he had been depressed. Farragut sat, day after day, pining to be at sea.

Now in January 1862, he was both promoted to flag officer and given the most important and thrilling assignment of his career. The success of his mission would give the Union a nearly complete blockade of the South. Then it would be only a matter of time before the Confederacy would come to an end. It was the chance of a lifetime.

Farragut was determined to live up to the hopes of his superiors. He was also as excited as a midshipman getting his first ship assignment. Shortly after his meeting with Fox he sat down and wrote a letter to his wife that revealed his excitement:

"Keep your lips closed and burn my letters, for perfect silence is to be observed—the first injunction of the Secretary. I am to have a flag in the Gulf, and the rest depends upon myself. Keep calm and silent. I shall sail in three weeks."

THE BATTLE OF NEW ORLEANS

"Success is the only thing listened to in this war,
and I know that I must sink or swim by that
rule."

FLAG OFFICER DAVID FARRAGUT

n February 2, 1862, the *Hartford*, a mighty 22-gun sloop equipped with both sails and steam power, set off for the Gulf of Mexico and Louisiana. The *Hartford* was 225 feet long and 44 feet wide. It was built of wood in Boston in 1858, along with three similar ships, the *Brooklyn*, the *Richmond*, and the *Pensacola*. The *Hartford* was to be flagship of a mighty fleet. The flag officer of the fleet stood on deck in his navy blue uniform, gazing at his future. His leathery skin showed him to be well-acquainted with the harsh life of the sea. His hair was gray and his face was lined with wrinkles, but his eyes sparkled with childlike eagerness.

The flag officer was known as a friendly, kindhearted man who could nevertheless dispatch an enemy with ruthless efficiency. The United States government was now putting its faith in him. On January 9, 1862, he had been appointed commander of the Western Gulf blockading squadron. His command extended from Florida to the Rio Grande in Texas.

David Farragut had carefully reviewed the plan of attack that the secretary of war had issued to him. Every step was vital. He would be in command of 18 warships, sloops and gunboats, all steam-powered and fully armed. But they were all wooden vessels. Farragut was an "old dog," who had little patience for the newfangled ironclad ships. "When a shell makes its way into one of those damn teakettles, it can't get out again," he once said. "It sputters around inside doing all kinds of mischief."

In addition to his 18 ships, there would also be a contingent of mortar boats, slow-moving converted schooners—a kind of sail-boat—which would toss heavy mortar shells into the forts guard-ing the river banks to the south of New Orleans. (A mortar is a short-range cannon.) Commander Porter was in charge of these. All told, there were 700 men under Farragut's command.

The Union assembled a formidable navy in a hurry by offering good pay and prizes.

A short time after they had assembled, the men became devoted to their leader. "Every one respects him, and our men will fight to the death for him," wrote a newspaper correspondent who accompanied the *Hartford*. It was common throughout the war for correspondents to view battles from shipboard.

As for Farragut himself, he was ready for the challenge. He wrote to his wife:

"I have now attained what I have been looking for all my life—a flag—and, having attained it, all that is necessary to complete the same is a victory. If I die in the attempt it will only be what every officer has to expect. He who dies in doing his duty to his country, and at peace with his God, has played out the drama of life to the best advantage. The great men in our country must not only plan but execute. Success is the only thing listened to in this war, and I know that I must sink or swim by that rule."

The plan to strike at New Orleans from the south was a bold one. It was as if the Confederates were guarding a house and watching from all the doors and windows except the cellar door, which was bricked up. Farragut's job was to find a way into that door. Then the house would be his for the taking.

The first task was to get the boats into the Mississippi River. This in itself was a gigantic effort. The water level at the mouth of the river, where the Mississippi fed into the Gulf of Mexico, was too low for the largest ships to pass through. The only possibility was to drag them through the silted (mud-clogged) passage. For the men to drag just one ship, the *Pensacola*, across the shoals took two weeks of back-breaking work.

It was mid-April by the time the fleet was assembled in the river. Now Farragut's orders were to proceed to the two forts that guarded the river just south of the city. Secretary Welles instructed him to bomb the forts into surrender, and then move on to take the city. But Farragut never liked this part of the plan. He did not think the fleet, sitting in a swift current, would be able to subdue the forts. He thought it made much more sense to race past the forts to the city itself. Then the fleet could bomb the city into submission, and the forts, cut off from the rest of the South, would have to surrender.

David Dixon Porter, Farragut's stepbrother, was in fact the mastermind of the strategy to take the forts first. For this reason he was appointed commander of the mortar ships, which were 20 schooners, each of which carried a 13-inch mortar. So although he and Farragut were long-time friends, they disagreed on how the battle ought to be fought.

But orders were orders. Farragut proceeded to carry them out to the best of his ability. On April 18, 1862, the fleet was anchored in position. At 10 A.M. the first mortar shells sang through the air, blasting inside Fort Jackson on the west side of the river, and Fort St. Philip on the east. The bombardment continued relentlessly, one shell a minute. The 1,400 Confederate troops within the forts suffered terribly. Huge stone walls were reduced to rubble. But somehow the forts were able to hold back the attackers.

During the bombardment, Farragut's crews were busy. The Confederates had constructed a barrier north of the forts to block the ships from passing. Farragut sent two sleek gunboats out late at night to cut through the chains that held the barrier together. Captain Henry Bell, commanding the squadron, carried out his mission with precision.

On April 20, Farragut made a decision. The forts showed no sign of surrendering, and the fleet was beginning to run low on ammunition. He would personally take responsibility for changing the secretary of the navy's orders. The fleet would try to run past the forts to the city.

One man objected strongly to this revised plan. David Dixon Porter thought it would be impossible to get the whole fleet, including the mortar ships, safely past the forts. What was more, there was almost certainly a fleet of Confederate ships waiting to block their path. They would be caught between the forts and the town.

But Farragut was flag officer and he had made up his mind. He ordered the ships to prepare to run past the forts. In a unique military move, the crews crisscrossed the wooden hulls with great chain ropes until they were almost as well protected as ironclads.

Next, since they would make their runs at night, Farragut ordered the ships' hulls covered with mud from the Mississippi to make them less visible from the shores. He also had the decks painted white, so that objects the men needed would stand out clearly in outline. Commander Porter was especially worried about his slow-moving mortar boats. He received permission to carry out a bizarre plan of his own. He had tall trees lashed to the masts of his vessels so that the men on shore would think they were trees on the opposite bank.

At last, at 2 A.M. on April 24, two red lanterns flashed briefly against the blackness of the night. This was the signal to move out. In the darkness it was difficult for Farragut, aboard the *Hartford*, to see the other ships, but he heard the grunts of men and the clinking of chain as anchors were weighed. Then the lead ship, the *Cayuga*, started off.

"Although it was a starlight night we were not discovered until well under the forts," said Lieutenant Perkins, commander of the *Cayuga*. "Then they opened upon us a tremendous fire."

The sky lit up red and yellow as Confederate shells rained down on the river. Great splashes of water rose up where shells burst on the sea. A sickening crack echoed over the water as a shell tore through a mast and the tall structure sailed down like a tree and crashed on the deck.

Once the passage was discovered, Commander Porter ordered his mortars to open fire on the forts again. Once again their great booming sounded in the air.

"The *Cayuga* received the first fire," Lieutenant Perkins said, "and the air was filled with shells and explosives which almost blinded me as I stood on the forecastle trying to see my way, for I had never been up the river before. I soon saw that the guns of the forts were all aimed for midstream, so I steered close under the walls of Fort St. Philip; and although our masts and rigging got badly shot through, our hull was but little damaged."

The little lead ship took the worst part of the assault, but kept moving. "After passing the last battery and thinking we were clear," Perkins said, "I looked back for some of our vessels, and my heart jumped up into my mouth when I found I could not see a single one. I thought they all must have been sunk by the forts."

The job of running gunpowder to the ships' guns was left to boys called powder monkeys.

In fact, the other ships were slowed down but not lost. As they passed by the forts the Confederate ships met them head on. Now the battle heated up. The air was thick with smoke, so that visibility more than a few feet away was impossible. One ship rammed into another with a dull thud and a splintering of wood. The Confederates were now sending blazing rafts of fire down the river toward the Union ships. "The river and its banks were one sheet of flame," wrote the correspondent aboard the *Hartford*.

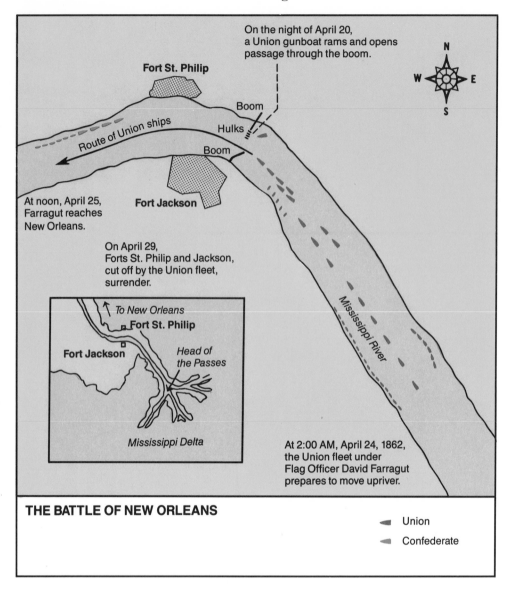

On the night of April 20, a Union gunboat rams and opens passage through the boom.

Fort St. Philip

Boom

Hulks

Route of Union ships

Boom

At noon, April 25, Farragut reaches New Orleans.

Fort Jackson

On April 29, Forts St. Philip and Jackson, cut off by the Union fleet, surrender.

To New Orleans

Fort St. Philip

Fort Jackson

Head of the Passes

Mississippi River

Mississippi Delta

At 2:00 AM, April 24, 1862, the Union fleet under Flag Officer David Farragut prepares to move upriver.

THE BATTLE OF NEW ORLEANS

◄ Union

◄ Confederate

"The smoke was so dense that it was only now and then we could see anything but the flash of the cannon and the blaze of the fire rafts," Farragut wrote later. "The passing of Forts Jackson and St. Philip was one of the most awful sights I ever saw."

Francis Roe, lieutenant aboard the *Pensacola*, agreed. "The groans, shrieks, and wails of the dying and wounded were so horrible that I shudder now at the recollection of it," he wrote later.

The worst moment came when Farragut realized with horror that the *Hartford* had been rammed by a fire raft. Instantly the flames licked up the sides of the wooden vessel, devouring the mast and rigging. The fire skitted across the deck. Suddenly it seemed that all was lost: the flagship was burning.

Farragut stood in the midst of the leaping flames. His face black from smoke, he shouted orders at the sailors, who scurried everywhere frantically with water buckets. With the aid of another ship, the crew of the *Hartford* finally brought the fire under control.

Despite the many near disasters, the Union forces kept up a steady shelling on the enemy ships and forts. By dawn they were past the forts and sailing on toward New Orleans. Behind them lay the twisted and destroyed remains of their assault on the Confederate fleet. Farragut had lost 37 men, and 149 were wounded. The two forts suffered 11 killed and 37 wounded. The Confederate ships had 73 dead and 73 wounded. Ten Confederate warships were sunk or burned in the battle.

The victory was complete. The forts were still manned, but flag officer Farragut felt certain they would surrender once he accomplished the next step: the occupation of New Orleans.

Fifty years after little David Farragut came from Lake Pontchartrain to the big city of New Orleans with his new guardian, Commander David Porter, flag officer David Farragut returned at the head of a victorious fleet. At noon on April 25, 1862, the weary fleet dropped anchor in the harbor.

Greeting them was quite a site. All up and down the Mississippi the banks and docks were jammed with a boiling mass of people. Every member of that crowd was raising a fist, waving a knife, or hollering hateful curses. They cheered Jefferson Davis, president of the Confederacy, and the Rebel flag. They shouted out their hatred for Abraham Lincoln, for the Union fleet, and for David Farragut.

Standing on the burnt deck of the *Hartford*, Farragut viewed the crowd. He felt no anger or hatred toward them. They were expressing their anger at defeat. Farragut knew the intense emo-

By taking New Orleans, Farragut won control of the Gulf of Mexico for the Union navy.

tions that war brings out. If he felt anything for the people of New Orleans who stood cursing him, it was sadness.

Always the crisp, efficient officer, Farragut picked two men to go on an important mission. Theodorus Bailey, captain of the *Cayuga*, and Lieutenant Perkins left their ship, approached the crowd, and politely asked the way to the mayor's office. They then set off down a street, and the furious mob closed in after them. Neither was armed.

"They were all shouting and hooting as we stepped on shore," Perkins wrote later. "As we advanced, the mob followed us in a very exciting state.... Then they began to throw things at us, and shout, 'Hang them! Hang them!' We both thought we were in a bad fix."

One of the young men in the crowd later wrote, "So through the gates of death those two men walked to the City Hall, to demand the town's surrender. It was one of the bravest deeds I ever saw done."

On April 28, the forts on the river surrendered to the Union fleet. The next day, the flag of the Confederacy was taken down from the flag pole at City Hall. The United States flag went up in its place. New Orleans was now in Union hands. The victory was a great emotional boost in Washington and throughout the North. Further, the French emperor Napoleon III had been on the verge of aiding the South in its cause. England had also considered helping the Confederacy. The fall of New Orleans prevented the European powers from openly intervening in the Civil War.

With the fall of New Orleans went control of the Gulf of Mexico. To the north, the Mississippi River stood open before Farragut's forces. It was a wide highway to the interior of the South.

CONFEDERATE DERRING-DO

"England should be held accountable for these outrages."

GIDEON WELLES, UNION SECRETARY OF THE NAVY

The South had lost its biggest city, but it was far from beaten. Stonewall Jackson, the flamboyant Confederate general, was marching up the Shenendoah Valley. As he went, he crushed invading Union armies in his path. Soon General Robert E. Lee would take his army across the Potomac River and invade the North.

Even along the Mississippi there was a slight chance of hope for the South. After his victory at New Orleans, flag officer Farragut brought his fleet 400 miles upriver to fire on the Confederate stronghold of Vicksburg, Mississippi. But Vicksburg was too powerful. Farragut's ships had to abandon their attack and fall back to New Orleans.

As 1862 wore on, things did not look so bad for the Rebel forces. The great Confederate generals were doing their jobs well. And in addition to the victories on land, the most glorious days of the ragtag Confederate navy were still in the future.

One rainy spring morning, several dark figures moved silently along the docks in Liverpool, England. These were agents of the United States government, on a spying mission. But their goal was not a person. It was a ship. Here, far from the battle cries that rang out across the American landscape, the shipbuilding firm of Laird Brothers was putting the finishing touches on a vessel the Union spies believed would be a warship for the South.

And it was no ordinary ship. A trim 200-foot-long vessel, powered by both sails and powerful steam engines, it looked like a magnificent arrow that would zip across the ocean. There was no doubting it was built for speed. But the Union spies had also discovered that it was built for war. True, there were no guns, which would have violated England's neutrality. But those holes in its sides could only have been meant for gun mountings.

As spring turned into summer, the agents sent worrisome messages to the capitol. First they learned that none other than James Bulloch, the shrewd Confederate naval expert, had arrived in Liverpool. Then came a more shocking report. A thin, fancy dresser who walked around like a prince and wore a large waxed mustache had been sighted in Liverpool. He was Captain Raphael Semmes, a former U.S. naval officer, a son of Alabama, who was as well-known for his hatred of Yankees as for his daring at sea. Semmes was now the most feared Confederate sea captain. He had sunk many Union merchant ships.

In midsummer, before the Union diplomats could effectively protest to the British government, the sleek vessel steamed out of the Liverpool harbor. The North's sea trade was about to be destroyed.

The ship was christened the *Alabama*. The story of the *Alabama*, the mustacchioed Captain Semmes, and its crew of tough English sailors, would be passed from one generation of seamen to the next for decades. For nearly two years, this one ship would, almost singlehandedly, cripple Union shipping around the world.

From England, the *Alabama* steamed off for distant parts of the globe. It went to Brazil, Africa, India, and the faraway Spice Islands, which today are part of the nation of Indonesia. Before the *Alabama* left England, Captain Semmes gathered his crew and explained the true purpose of their mission, which had been kept secret. They would roam the globe, searching for United States merchant ships to destroy.

With powerful words Semmes painted a picture that the rough sailors could understand. He told them that England was the home of justice, and that as British sailors they would be defending the justice of the South against the Northern oppressors. He called upon them, as good Englishmen, to help defend the cause of freedom. Then he promised them lots of money. The crew loved him.

Less than two weeks after they left England, the *Alabama*'s crew became part of the Civil War. They met up with their first Union merchant ship on September 5, 1862. The crew worked swiftly and cleanly. They fired a shot across the ship's bow, boarded it, put the captured crew ashore on an island, took as many supplies as they could, then burned the ship by the light of dawn.

So went the first of an amazing number of captures. Within a short time, the name Semmes became a curse in the North. He was like an evil spirit that could appear anywhere on earth to destroy Union shipping. Citizens of New York, Baltimore, and Pittsburgh read how he severely damaged Union trade in the Caribbean. Then he turned up far down the coast of Brazil. Next he appeared off the coast of South Africa. Everywhere he went, he left a trail of burned supply ships.

Over the course of the war, the South would send off many "patriotic pirates" to spoil Union trade. But Captain Semmes and the *Alabama*, alone, were responsible for over half of all the damage. The *Alabama* captured 62 Union vessels in all, during the war. It had cost $200,000 to build the *Alabama*, but it inflicted over $3,000,000 worth of damage. This one ship nearly brought trade in the North to a standstill.

As the death toll of Union vessels rose, navy secretary Gideon Welles became furious. "England should be held accountable for these outrages," he raged. He sent ship after ship to find and destroy the *Alabama*. But nobody could seem to locate it. The *Alabama* was like a dream ship.

In addition to raiders, the Confederate navy outfitted a number of other special ships. As the war continued and the Union blockade cut off the South from supplies, special ships known as

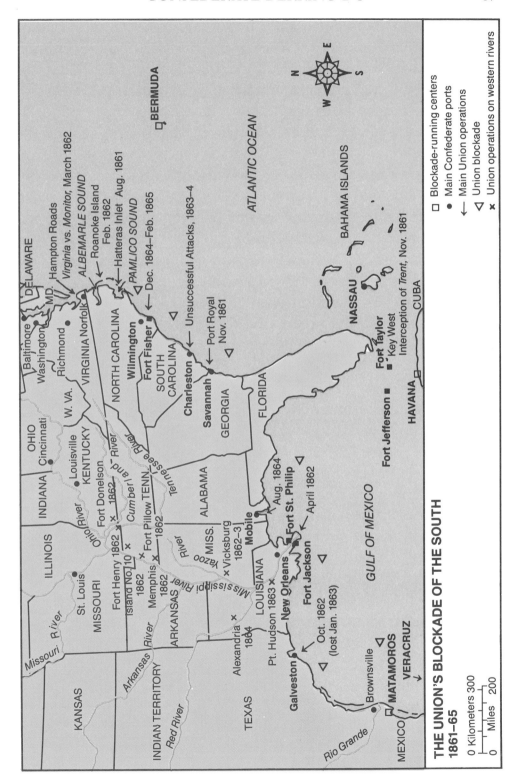

**THE UNION'S BLOCKADE OF THE SOUTH
1861–65**

☐ Blockade-running centers
● Main Confederate ports
→ Main Union operations
▽ Union blockade
✕ Union operations on western rivers

blockade runners became vitally important. These vessels, piloted by very skilled captains, would slip past the mighty Union warships that kept guard over the Southern coasts. This was precisely the tactic of many American vessels during the War of 1812, when England had been doing the blockading.

While Confederate sailors were doing their best against the superior Union navy, President Jefferson Davis was trying to find other ways of helping the South. His chief diplomat, James Mason, traveled to England to convince the British to openly support the Confederate cause. Southern leaders believed this would happen eventually, because England depended so heavily on cotton. Eighty percent of England's cotton came from the Southern states.

One Southern leader was so certain of the power of "King Cotton" that he announced that if England did not break the blockade and aid the Confederacy, "England would topple head-long and carry the whole civilized world with her, save the South."

For a time it looked as if the Southerners would be right. England's foreign secretary, Lord John Russell, instructed his ambassador in Washington to secretly allow Confederate represent-atives to come to London to meet with him. "I shall see the Southerners when they come," he said, "but not officially. And keep them at a proper distance."

Late in 1862, when the war was going well for the Confederacy, Lord Palmerston, Britain's prime minister, declared to Parliament, "We may anticipate with certainty the success of the Southern states, so far as regards their separation from the North."

The other major European power was France. Emperor Napoleon III met with John Slidell, the South's representative in France. The emperor expressed interest in supporting the Con-federacy if things continued to progress in the South's favor.

But things would soon change. On September 22, 1862, Abraham Lincoln issued the Emancipation Proclamation. This document decreed that beginning January 1, 1863, all slaves in the rebelling Southern states and western territories would become free. Of course, it was impossible for the president to enforce the proclamation. He was busy fighting the South. Logically, he could not expect Southerners to obey his command and release their slaves while they were in the middle of a war.

Still, the Emancipation Proclamation had an important effect in Europe. Now the Union officially supported the abolition of slavery. It would not look good for European governments to side with the South, which maintained such a barbarous practice. All talks between Confederate and European diplomats came to an end. There would be no aid from Europe.

The Confederacy would have to win the war on its own. From now on, the South relied even more heavily on its courageous sea pilots and their daring crews.

Still, there was one more crisis to come between England and the United States. After secretly allowing the *Alabama* to be built by the Laird Brothers, the British had agreed to build two more ships. These were ironclad war vessels equipped with deadly iron rams. If these ships became part of the South's navy, they could destroy the entire Union fleet.

When Northern spies sent word of the construction of these vessels to Secretary Welles, he panicked. "We have no defense against them," he wrote. "It is a matter of life and death."

The United States' cool, dignified ambassador to Great Britain, Charles Francis Adams, immediately went to work. He sent Lord Russell, the British foreign secretary, a short note that contained a threat: "It would be superfluous in me to point out to your Lordship that this is war." Adams was gently telling the British official that his government was prepared to consider shipbuilding for the South an act of war against the United States.

Lord Russell understood. The two ironclad rams were sold to the British navy. The nations of Europe would no longer aid the Confederacy.

THE UNION INCHES AHEAD

"We have done our part of the work assigned to
us, and all has worked well."

FARRAGUT, AFTER THE FALL OF VICKSBURG

The year 1863 was the turning point in the Civil War, both on land and at sea. On the Mississippi River, David Farragut's fleet failed to take the crucial city of Vicksburg, Mississippi. But now a new strategy was in place. Union armies were marching toward the river. A combined assault was in the works.

It was an eventful time for Farragut. On July 16, 1862, just two months after the glorious Union victory at New Orleans, he was promoted to rear admiral, the highest rank in the navy, along with three other officers. Since Farragut was the most senior of the officers, his promotion came first. And, since the rank had only just been created, David Farragut became the first rear admiral in the history of the United States Navy.

But things were not all easy. Following the New Orleans victory, a variety of illnesses swept over his ships. Farragut himself was bedridden for several weeks, fuming the whole time at his inability to help the Union. Concerned about the blockade along the Gulf of Mexico, he then moved most of his fleet to Pensacola, Florida. He was pleased to learn that the Union navy commanded the entire Gulf Coast, except for the wide bay of Mobile, Alabama. This, Farragut knew, would be the next major target.

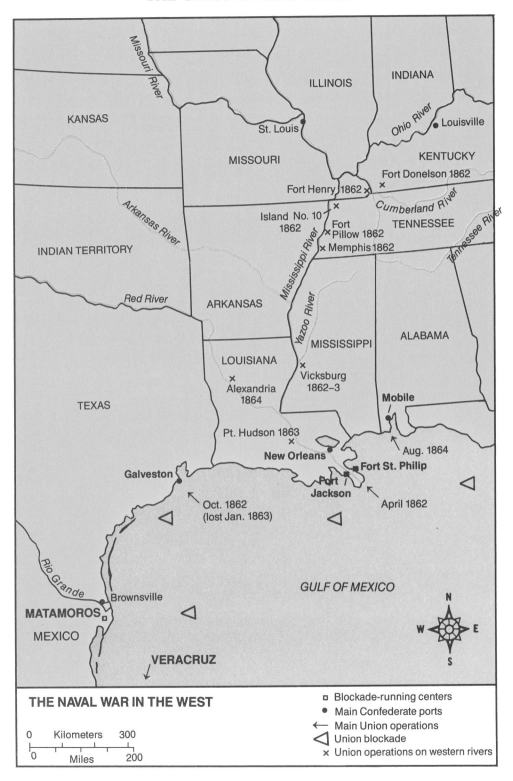

KANSAS

MISSOURI

ILLINOIS

INDIANA

St. Louis

Ohio River

Louisville

KENTUCKY

Fort Donelson 1862 ×

Fort Henry 1862 ×

Island No. 10 1862 ×

Cumberland River

TENNESSEE

Fort Pillow 1862 ×

Memphis 1862 ×

Tennessee River

INDIAN TERRITORY

Arkansas River

Red River

ARKANSAS

Mississippi River

Yazoo River

MISSISSIPPI

ALABAMA

LOUISIANA

× Alexandria 1864

× Vicksburg 1862–3

Mobile

TEXAS

Pt. Hudson 1863 ×

New Orleans

Aug. 1864

Fort St. Philip

Galveston

Oct. 1862 (lost Jan. 1863)

Fort Jackson

April 1862

Rio Grande

Brownsville

MATAMOROS

MEXICO

GULF OF MEXICO

N
W   E
S

VERACRUZ

THE NAVAL WAR IN THE WEST

0   Kilometers   300

0   Miles   200

▫ Blockade-running centers
● Main Confederate ports
← Main Union operations
◁ Union blockade
× Union operations on western rivers

But first, there was the Mississippi. The Union high command wanted it. Farragut wanted it, too. But it would take a combination of land and sea forces to win the river. David Dixon Porter, now in command of his mortar flotilla farther north, moved on Vicksburg. Farragut headed north from Baton Rouge to meet up with him. But this time, the river was not so easy to navigate. The town of Port Hudson, Louisiana, had fortified itself. It was determined not to let the Union navy have its way.

Admiral Farragut led his fleet in a brilliant pass of the Port Hudson troops. Always clever at inventing strategies to deal with the situation, Farragut employed a new tactic.

The Port Hudson guns were positioned all along one side of the river. Half of Farragut's ships were heavy, slow steamers with lots of firepower. The other half were light, easily maneuverable vessels. Farragut ordered them to pass in pairs, with each large ship facing the Port Hudson batteries. This way the large ships could direct their guns on the batteries while the smaller ships would be protected, but would still be ready to fire if needed. Also, if a large ship were hit, the smaller one could tow it away safely.

Farragut directed the operation from the quarterdeck of the *Hartford*. He issued a detailed general order to his captains. Among the instructions he said, "The best protection against the enemy's fire is a well-directed fire from our own guns."

The fleet passed the batteries with only one casualty. The mighty frigate *Mississippi* ran aground just opposite the batteries and was sunk. But Farragut got the rest of his fleet past the Confederate guns. He pushed on to seal off the mouth of the Red River.

This was a crucial step. Farragut had blocked off the southern Mississippi and the Red River. The vital Confederate supply line from the West was cut off. "I look upon it as of vast importance that we should hold the river securely between Vicksburg and Port Hudson," wrote the man Farragut was soon to join, the Union general, Ulysses S. Grant. Grant's army was now preparing for a land assault further upriver on Vicksburg. Grant deeply appreciated Farragut's bold maneuver in closing off the southern waterways.

Meanwhile, Grant's opponent, the Confederate general Pemberton, whose job it was to hold Port Hudson and Vicksburg, did not know what to do. "The Mississippi is again cut off," he wrote to his superiors. "Neither subsistence nor ordnance can come or go."

Farragut, with only two ships, the *Hartford* and the *Albatross*, pushed on upriver toward Vicksburg. He was deep in Southern territory now. At his side on the quarterdeck of the *Hartford* was his 19-year-old son, Loyall, serving as his aide.

All along the riverbanks Farragut found stores of supplies for Confederate ships. These he confiscated or destroyed.

By May, General Grant's forces had crossed the Mississippi River from Louisiana into the state of Mississippi. They were within striking distance of Vicksburg. Porter prepared his ships for the assault. He was to be the naval commander of the operation. The Mississippi River was now in his hands. Farragut's responsibility was the blockade of the Gulf. Having done all he could, he headed back toward New Orleans.

Faced with continuous bombardment from Porter's fleet and Grant's land assault, the city of Vicksburg fell on July 4, 1863. The fortress at Port Hudson surrendered on July 9. Farragut's actions had cut off the Confederate supply of food and other needed goods, and he had assisted General Grant in his attack. Farragut felt pride at his role. "We have done our part of the work assigned to us," he wrote to his wife, "and all has worked well. My last dash past Port Hudson was the best thing I ever did, except taking New Orleans. It assisted materially in the fall of Vicksburg and Port Hudson."

The strongest Confederate post on the southern Mississippi had fallen. The noose was tightening.

While the Union forces were sealing off the western Confederacy, the greatest and one of the most vicious battles of the war was taking place in the East. Southern armies headed by Robert E. Lee had stormed northward into Pennsylvania. There, in the town of Gettysburg, they faced the Union's Major General George Meade.

For three days the rival armies battled one another across muddy fields. At times, the air was so thick with bullets that two bullets would collide. General Lee, sensing that Union armies were inching ahead in all arenas of the war, pushed for an all-out attack on the great Army of the Potomac.

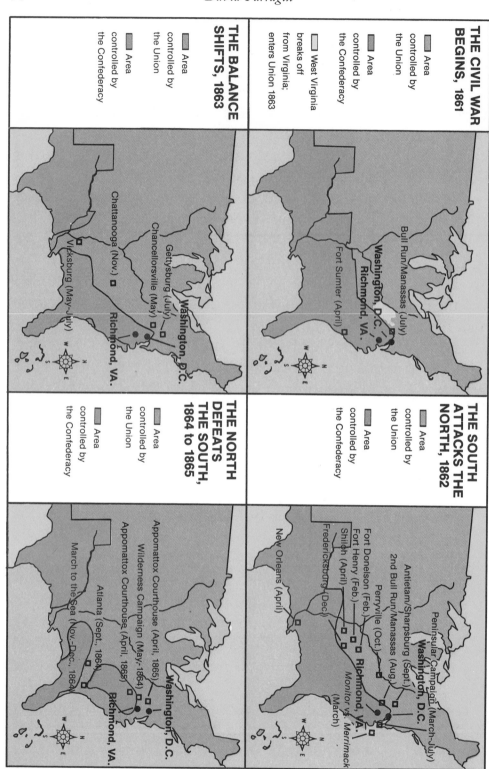

THE CIVIL WAR BEGINS, 1861

■ Area controlled by the Union

■ Area controlled by the Confederacy

☐ West Virginia breaks off from Virginia; enters Union 1863

Fort Sumter (April)

Bull Run/Manassas (July)

Washington, D.C.

Richmond, VA.

THE SOUTH ATTACKS THE NORTH, 1862

■ Area controlled by the Union

■ Area controlled by the Confederacy

Peninsular Campaign (March–July)

Antietam/Sharpsburg (Sept.)

2nd Bull Run/Manassas (Aug.)

Perryville (Oct.)

Fort Donelson (Feb.)

Fort Henry (Feb.)

Shiloh (April)

Fredericksburg (Dec.)

New Orleans (April)

Washington, D.C.

Richmond, VA.

Monitor vs. Merrimack (March)

THE BALANCE SHIFTS, 1863

■ Area controlled by the Union

■ Area controlled by the Confederacy

Vicksburg (May–July)

Chattanooga (Nov.)

Gettysburg (July)

Chancellorsville (May)

Washington, D.C.

Richmond, VA.

THE NORTH DEFEATS THE SOUTH, 1864 to 1865

■ Area controlled by the Union

■ Area controlled by the Confederacy

Appomattox Courthouse (April, 1865)

Wilderness Campaign (May–1864)

Appomattox Courthouse, (April, 1865)

Atlanta (Sept. 1864)

March to the Sea (Nov.–Dec. 1864)

Washington, D.C.

Richmond, VA.

After the first day of battle, it seemed Lee's strategy would work. The Confederate troops crushed the smaller Union army. The fighting came to a furious climax on the third day. General George Pickett led 15,000 men in his famous charge up Cemetery Hill. At the top of the ridge, dug into position in a stand of trees, sat the Union soldiers. When the Southerners got close enough, Union guns blasted away. Smoke filled the air. General Lee, watching from a nearby hill, could not see what was happening.

The charge failed. The scattered Rebel soldiers fled back to their lines. In three days of fighting, nearly 40,000 men died. The Battle of Gettysburg was over. In that one week the South lost the Mississippi River and the major battle of the East.

Then, in June 1864, the South lost its prized sea vessel. The *Alabama*, which had roamed the globe destroying Union shipping, was about to meet its match.

The dashing Captain Semmes and his brave crew had completed nearly two years of destroying enemy ships. Now, worn and weary, the *Alabama* steamed into the port of Cherbourg, France, for rest and repairs. The Union ship *Kearsarge*, one of many that had been searching for the *Alabama*, got word of the raider's presence in France and sailed to meet it. With a summer drizzle clouding the water, Captain John Winslow finally pulled his ship within sight of the *Alabama*.

The *Alabama*'s crew was excited. So was Captain Semmes. The Union vessel, by lying in wait at the mouth of the harbor, was challenging them to a duel. It would be an affair of honor between two noble equals. Winslow and Semmes had been friends at one time. They had served aboard ship together back in the Mexican War. Now they would meet in combat. Semmes, the "pirate captain" with the heart of a nobleman, accepted the challenge.

On the morning of June 19, 1864, the duel began. Half the population of Cherbourg was ranged along the coast to watch. In the harbor were many pleasure boats owned by wealthy Parisians who had come out to watch the fight.

It was an exciting moment. The citizens of France had long read accounts of the vicious battles taking place in the American Civil

War. They knew the outcome would decide the fate of the continent, and of much of the world. Here was their chance to witness one of the great battles right off their own coast.

The battle began with the two ships exchanging cannon fire as they slowly circled one another. They began about a half-mile apart, and gradually came closer. Suddenly a shell tore through the rigging of the *Kearsarge*. The crowd gasped. Then a great shell exploded into the hull of the *Kearsarge*. Amazingly, it did not appear to do much damage.

Then it was the Union vessel's turn to attack. One shot brought down the main mast, with the Confederate flag atop it. Shells exploded on deck, tearing gaping holes. The sailors scattered. Soon the deck was slick with blood and the water bobbed with corpses of the dead.

Then one great blast sounded, deafening the sailors still at their posts. A deep cracking sound followed. Then silence. The crew looked at one another, blood streaking their clothes and a look of confusion on their faces. The *Alabama* was about to go down.

Captain Semmes ordered the white flag of surrender run up the mizzenmast. The men filled the small boats, scurrying to get away before the *Alabama* sank. Meanwhile, Captain Winslow saw the flag and sent his small boats to help round up men who were floundering in the water. A few minutes later, he sighed with satisfaction as he watched the *Alabama* sink, stern first. The only task left was to round up the prisoners. Winslow was especially eager to get the prisoner named Semmes.

But he never did. One of the wealthy yachtsmen was an Englishman who supported the Confederates. He came alongside the sinking vessel to help round up survivors. Seeing Captain Semmes, the yachtsman picked him up, along with several of his officers, and slipped away before Captain Winslow knew what happened.

So ended the amazing career of the raider *Alabama*. The ship had done its utmost to destroy Union trade. But the work of the raiders was not enough to upset the powerful and well-manned Union navy. With men like David Farragut and David Dixon Porter in charge, the Northern blockade was secure.

THE BATTLE OF MOBILE BAY

"Damn the torpedoes! Full speed ahead!"
ADMIRAL FARRAGUT

In 1864, Northerners had mixed feelings about the war. They knew they had won many important victories. But they also feared that Southerners would continue fighting no matter how desperate their situation became. It was like the War of 1812 in some ways. Then, Britain had the mightier army, but the Americans were determined to continue fighting, no matter what the odds. Finally, the American determination forced a peace treaty.

Many Northerners felt the war had gone on long enough. It should be ended by a truce, they said, even if it meant giving the South what it wanted. The coming presidential election would decide the matter. If Lincoln won, it would be a vote of confidence in his leadership. If he lost, however, it might mean that the Union would be forced to offer terms for a truce. Many thought this would be a disgrace to the memory of all the brave soldiers and sailors who had died fighting to preserve the Union.

Then came a stunning event at sea—the battle for Mobile Bay. This battle put the last Confederate stronghold on the Gulf in Union hands. Suddenly, people in the North once again began to think about winning.

Mobile was a target that David Farragut had wanted to attack right after his victory at New Orleans in April 1862. But his superiors in Washington ordered him to concentrate on the Mississippi. Now, two years later, Mobile Bay was heavily defended. It would be much more difficult to take. Still, it had to be done.

It was January 1864. Farragut was back in New York, having finished his work in the West. Finally he got word that Washington wanted Mobile Bay taken. There was no doubt who should lead the fleet. Lincoln and his advisors turned to the gray-haired, dignified old salt who had punched open the Mississippi. Rear Admiral Farragut sailed south that very week for the Gulf of Mexico, where he would assemble his fleet. He had waited two years for this. He planned to attack at once.

January went by, with no attack on Mobile Bay. The Union high command had decided that Farragut should be supported by an army force, but none was available. Farragut was furious at the delay. He settled into a dull routine in New Orleans, slowly assembling his fleet and getting gloomy reports on the progress of the war in other arenas, where the Southerners were making courageous stands.

These reports only made his mood worse. "I am depressed by the bad news from every direction," he wrote to his wife. "The enemy seem to be bending their whole soul and body to the war and whipping us in every direction. What a disgrace that, with their slender means, they should, after three years, contend with us from one end of the country to the other!"

Later, he managed to chuckle at a newspaper report that declared that if David Farragut won Mobile Bay he should run for president. "As if a man who had toiled up the ladder of life for fifty-two years and reached the top round in his profession did not need a little rest," he wrote home. "My own opinion is that, if I survive these two engagements, there is little doubt that a presidential campaign would finish me. No, after I have finished my work, I hope to be allowed to spend the remainder of my days in peace and quiet with my family on the banks of the Hudson."

Finally, in June, he got some war news that pleased him very much. The report came in that the *Kearsarge* had found the dreaded Confederate raider *Alabama* and sunk it. Farragut envied Captain Winslow of the *Kearsarge* for his dramatic victory. "I would sooner have fought that fight than any ever fought on the ocean," he said.

While the months of waiting wore on, information about the Confederate presence at Mobile Bay trickled in. This consisted of a wooden fleet commanded by Admiral Franklin Buchanan, and the powerfully built Fort Morgan, which guarded the bay. However, it turned out that besides this the Rebels had a surprise. It was the *Tennessee*, an ironclad of unusual strength and firepower. It would be able to withstand the pounding of a whole fleet of wooden vessels, then slowly sink each!

Admiral Farragut wired Washington the news that if he was to take the bay he would need some ironclads of his own. "I feel no apprehension about Buchanan's raising the blockade," he wrote, "but, with such force as he has in the bay, it would be unwise to take in our wooden vessels without the means of fighting the enemy on an equal footing."

Eventually he got what he wanted. Four small ironclads were added to his fleet. These were of a different type than the *Tennessee*. The four Union vessels were called monitors. They were like little rounded forts stuck on rafts, covered with iron sheeting. The "fort" had a turret with a swivel gun in the center.

The *Tennessee*, by contrast, was an enormous thing, more than 200 feet long and nearly 50 feet wide. Its guns were ranged all along the sides, as in a warship, and all were heavy caliber, able to fire heavy shells. Its center rose up in a slanted iron wall. The slant protected it, for it made shot fired at it glance off rather than penetrate. Though it was slow and cumbersome, it was nearly indestructible.

For these reasons, Farragut was not completely at ease, even with the four monitors. He knew it was harder to attack than to defend, and required more firepower. But he did not worry too much about defeat. "Any man who is prepared for defeat is half-defeated before he commences," he wrote.

At last, in August 1864, all was ready. The land forces of General Gordon Granger were in place to take up the attack once the fleet had done its work. On the night before the battle, Admiral Farragut had a hard time getting to sleep. He had an odd feeling. He knew that this would be the final battle of his career. In his heart he felt he might not survive it. He wrote a letter to his wife that was full of love, for he thought he might never see her again:

Flag-ship Hartford
Off Mobile, August 4, 1864

My Dearest Wife:

I write and leave this letter for you. I am going into Mobile [Bay] in the morning, if God is my leader, as I hope he is, and in him I place my trust. If he thinks it is the proper place for me to die, I am ready to submit to his will in that as in all other things. My great mortification is that my vessels, the ironclads, were not ready to have gone in yesterday. The army landed last night, and are in full view of us this morning, and the Tecumseh has not yet arrived from Pensacola.
God bless and preserve you, my darling, and my dear boy, if anything should happen to me; and may his blessings also rest upon your dear mother, and all your sisters and their children.
Your devoted and affectionate husband, who never for one moment forgot his love, duty, or fidelity to you, his devoted and best of wives,
D.G. Farragut

At last Farragut dropped off to sleep. He slept for a few hours before being awakened by his assistant. It was not yet dawn but preparations were underway. The battle was about to begin.

On August 5, at 6:22 A.M., a great *BOOM!* sounded over Fort Morgan, startling the troops inside. The Union fleet was attacking!

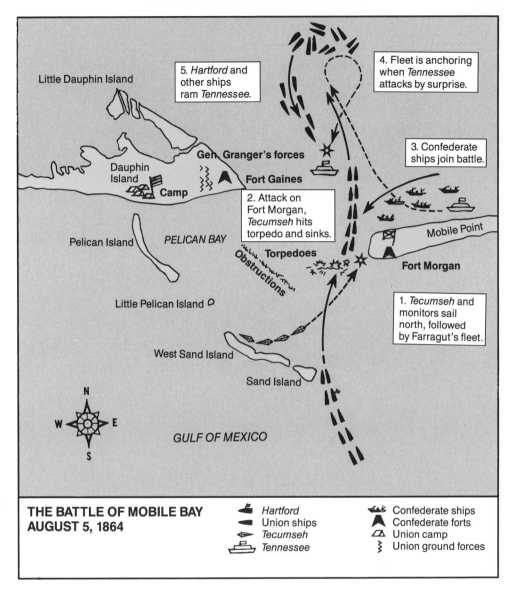

Little Dauphin Island

5. *Hartford* and other ships ram *Tennessee.*

4. Fleet is anchoring when *Tennessee* attacks by surprise.

Gen. Granger's forces

3. Confederate ships join battle.

Dauphin Island

Camp

Fort Gaines

2. Attack on Fort Morgan, *Tecumseh* hits torpedo and sinks.

Mobile Point

Pelican Island

PELICAN BAY

Obstructions Torpedoes

Fort Morgan

Little Pelican Island

1. *Tecumseh* and monitors sail north, followed by Farragut's fleet.

West Sand Island

Sand Island

N
W   E
S

GULF OF MEXICO

THE BATTLE OF MOBILE BAY
AUGUST 5, 1864

Hartford
Union ships
Tecumseh
Tennessee

Confederate ships
Confederate forts
Union camp
Union ground forces

Quickly the Confederate gunners got ready. They fired a return volley. From the ramparts they could see the entire fleet steaming toward them. The mission of Farragut's fleet was to run past the fort, just as he had done in the battle of New Orleans. Once clear of the fort, they would be in Mobile Bay itself. From there they could control the town and all sea traffic. The Confederacy's last major stronghold on the Gulf would be theirs.

The Rebels in the fort saw the enemy ships set out in a strange pattern. They were coming in pairs, with a large frigate and a smaller vessel lashed together. Farragut was using the same tactic that had worked so well at Port Hudson.

Meanwhile, Farragut himself directed the attack from the flagship *Hartford*. Shortly after the firing began, however, he found the smoke too thick to see through. Nimbly, the old sailor climbed up the main rigging for a better view. As the smoke rose higher, he climbed higher. Finally he was near the top of the mainsail, with the battle spread out beneath him.

The captain of the *Hartford* saw his admiral hanging like a boy from the rigging. He sent a sailor up to lash Farragut to the rigging with a rope. Farragut at first pushed him away, then finally let the sailor secure him.

Later a cartoon would appear in *Frank Leslie's Illustrated Newspaper* showing naval officers tied to the mainmast of their ships, leading an attack. "The illustrated papers are very amusing," Farragut would write. "Leslie has me lashed up to the mast like a culprit, and says, 'It is the way officers will hereafter go into battle, etc.'"

Leading the pairs of ships that approached Fort Morgan were the four monitors, looking like tanks on the water. The Rebel soldiers watched expectantly as the monitors came nearer. Suddenly there was a tremendous explosion. The first monitor, the *Tecumseh*, hit one of the mines that the Confederates had dropped at the mouth of the harbor. These mines, which in those days were called torpedoes, were set out in three rows to block the oncoming fleet.

Suddenly the *Tecumseh* gave a great groan and slipped beneath the surface. Nearly its entire crew went down. This caused immediate confusion among the other ships. The monitors slowed, and the ships behind were forced to slow down as well.

This was a disastrous situation. The fleet ground to a halt right in front of the guns of Fort Morgan. The Confederates knew the *Hartford* was the flagship, so they concentrated their fire on her. Shells blasted in on deck. Sailors watched in horror as men who stood beside them were blown to pieces. Heads, arms, and legs were torn from bodies.

Farragut, still watching from above, demanded to know why they had halted. The captain told him the ships were afraid of the torpedoes.

"Damn the torpedoes!" came Farragut's cry from above. "Full speed ahead!"

Slowly the fleet lurched forward. The monitors returned fire, pounding the fort relentlessly. Their gunnery crews worked like well-oiled machinery. There were no more explosions from the "torpedoes." They were crudely made and, as Farragut knew, often failed to work.

By 9 A.M. most of the fleet had made it past the fort and were anchored in the harbor. Cheers went up from the decks. But the battle was not over yet. No sooner had the men settled back to catch their breath than they saw an ominous object steaming toward them. Black as pitch, solid as a stone wall, the ironclad *Tennessee* was chugging into the harbor after them.

The *Tennessee* made for the *Hartford*, firing its guns as it neared. Farragut quickly ordered the ships into formation. One of his smaller crafts, the *Monongahela*, went on the attack with its battering ram. It flew headlong at the heavy ironclad, crashing into its side. But the *Tennessee* remained unharmed, while the *Monongahela* nearly splintered apart.

Now the *Hartford* opened fire with all its port guns. The *Lackawanna* did the same. Shells rained down on the *Tennessee* from every direction. Heavy shot rang off its sides. Its steering chains were shot away, so now it could not maneuver. The gun ports were blasted shut, so the ironclad's deadly guns could no longer fire. The smokestack was hit and fell with a crash.

Finally, at ten o'clock, a white flag appeared over the beaten hulk. A distant chorus of cheers went up from the Union fleet surrounding it. It had taken the whole fleet to beat the fearsome ironclad, but they had done it. They were now in the harbor. Mobile Bay, the last Gulf Coast stronghold of the Confederacy, was theirs.

The victory lightened the hearts of the whole Union. Suddenly, the Civil War seemed winnable. If Farragut could take Mobile Bay,

THE BATTLE OF MOBILE BAY

Mobile Bay was protected by Fort Morgan, a fleet of wooden vessels, and the powerful ironclad *Tennessee*. Admiral Farragut had his wooden ships lashed together in pairs. Then, aided by four small ironclads, his fleet began the attack. Farragut tied himself to the rigging of the *Hartford* for a better view of the battle. The *Tennessee* chugged, and Farragut ordered the *Hartford* to ram it. The *Hartford* shook with each ramming, but the ship's gunners continued to blast away at the ironclad. By ten o'clock on the morning of August 5, 1864, the *Tennessee* had had enough. The Confederate forces surrendered, and Mobile Bay, the last stronghold on the Gulf of Mexico, was in Union hands.

Admiral Farragut, hanging from the rigging of the *Hartford*, directs the attack on the *Tennessee*

After Mobile Bay, the ailing Farragut sailed home to New York in his trusty flagship

people said, perhaps Grant—the new commander-in-chief of the Union army—could win a series of important land battles that would bring the war to an end.

The victory had not come easily. The battle in Mobile Bay had taken its toll on the Union fleet. Nearly 200 Union sailors had died. Only 12 Confederates had died and 20 were wounded, but 243 men were captured. Most of Farragut's ships were badly damaged. One, the *Brooklyn*, had been hit by 59 shells and was nearly sunk.

The battle has also taken its toll on Admiral Farragut. He had been feeling drained for some time, and longed for his work to be finished. With his final battle over, the 63-year-old man was overcome with fatigue.

"I was talking to the admiral today," wrote one of Farragut's officers shortly after the battle, "when all at once he fainted away. He is not very well and is all tired out. It gave me quite a shock, and shows how exhausted he is, and his health is not very good, any way. He is a mighty fine old fellow."

Farragut himself understood his condition. In September a message arrived from Washington ordering him to take command of another attack. The old sailor shook his head. His strength would not last.

"I have been down in the Gulf five years out of six," he wrote to Secretary Welles, "with the exception of a short time at home last fall. The last six months have been a severe drag upon me, and I want rest, if it is to be had."

Welles quickly assigned another man to head the attack. The weary Admiral Farragut was called home. On November 30 he bid his fleet good-bye, and sailed northward in his trusty flagship, the *Hartford*. He was a hero to the men who had served under him, and to the whole nation. Now his role in the Civil War was complete.

The End of the Old Ways

"I suppose, General Grant, that the object of our
present meeting is fully understood. I asked to
see you to ascertain upon what terms you would
receive the surrender of my army."

GENERAL ROBERT E. LEE

ard, cold rain fell steadily on the evening of November 8,
1864. The streets of Washington, D.C., were flooded. The
White House sat silent. Across the street, however, a light
burned in the War Department telegraph office. Inside, a group of
men exchanged small talk and shifted nervously. The man in the
center, President Abraham Lincoln, tried to calm everyone by
reading humorous stories from an old book. Edwin Stanton, the
secretary of war, raised his eyebrows and fumed. He felt the
president was making too little of the occasion.

Occasionally the telegraph would start to chatter. Everyone would
sit up, awaiting the news. Another state was reporting the early
returns of the presidential election. A man kept a running tally.
Lincoln needed none, however: he kept his own tally in his head.

By midnight the men had enough returns to judge the result.
Abraham Lincoln had been reelected. The people had chosen to
continue his leadership, trusting him to bring the war to an end.

At two o'clock in the morning Lincoln got up and left the War
Office. Outside, the rain had stopped. A brass band stood in the

darkness to greet him with a rousing song. Lincoln told them, "It is no pleasure to me to triumph over any one; but I give thanks to the Almighty for this evidence of the people's resolution to stand by free government and the rights of humanity."

Three months later, on March 4, 1865, Lincoln delivered his second inaugural address:

> With malice toward none, with charity for all, with firmness in the right as God gives us to see the right, let us strive on to finish the work we are in, to bind up the nation's wounds, to care for him who shall have born the battle and for his widow and his orphan, to do all which may achieve and cherish a just and lasting peace among ourselves and with all nations.

The "work we are in" was soon finished. General George Thomas crushed the army of Confederate General John Hood in Tennessee. Sheridan swept through the Shenendoah. Generals Sherman and Grant marched with their armies closer and closer to the Confederate capital at Richmond.

By now Confederate commander-in-chief Robert E. Lee knew that the situation was almost hopeless. His valiant army of Northern Virginia was hungry, exhausted, and outnumbered. Facing him in a 40-mile arc around Petersburg, Virginia, was the fit and fine-tuned army of Ulysses S. Grant. On April 2, 1865, Grant mounted an all-out assault on the weakened Rebels. The Confederates were crushed, split into wandering, leaderless divisions.

The next day Union troops entered Richmond. The capital was a burning ghost town, most of its citizens gone. Before leaving, people had set fire to their stores of food rather than have them fall into Union hands. The Confederate government had also fled. A reporter from the *Boston Journal* wrote:

"The Capitol, outside and in, like the Confederacy, is exceedingly dilapidated. The windows are broken, the carpets faded, the paint dingy, the desks rickety."

Now Abraham Lincoln himself entered the city, saw the ruins of war, and entered the Rebel government's headquarters, where he sat

President Lincoln's second inauguration. Lincoln is in the very center of the picture.

at Jefferson Davis's desk. The president witnessed firsthand the final moments of the rebellion he had promised to put down.

General Lee managed to get his army together one last time, and led them in a fast march westward. By April 9, they could go no further. The two armies faced one another across a muddy field at Appomattox Court House. Union soldiers were preparing for a final attack when suddenly a cry went up. A single Confederate cavalryman was riding toward them holding aloft a white flag. Men looked around in bewilderment, hardly able to believe their eyes. The commander-in-chief of the Confederacy was surrendering.

The year 1865 brought many things to an end. With the surrender of Lee to Grant at Appomattox Court House, the Civil War was over. The hope of the South for a nation of its own came to an end. The bloodshed was ended, and healing would begin.

The year would also bring the tragic end of the Lincoln years. On April 14, 1865, less than a week after Lee's surrender, the president was in Washington attending a play at Ford's Theatre with his wife. Suddenly, a crazed actor named John Wilkes Booth burst into the president's stall and shot him in the head. He then leaped down onto the stage and dashed out into the night before anyone in the shocked crowd could react. He would be caught several days later.

The president was taken to a house across the street where he died the next morning. He had lived just long enough to see his nation victorious.

The year would also mean an end to many old ways of thinking for the citizens of the United States. No longer would they think of themselves as simple farmers far removed from the "advanced" and "modern" nations of Europe. The war had brought them into closer contact with the outside world. It had brought a new wave of technology that would reshape their lives in the coming decades.

In many ways the Civil War brought an end to the simplicity of the past. For the North, it brought victory. For the whole country, it brought change.

THE PARTYGOER

"This is the last time I shall ever tread the deck of
a man-of-war."

ADMIRAL DAVID FARRAGUT

he *Hartford* sailed into New York harbor on December 12,
1864. The war was still being fought, but the citizens of
New York lined the docks and cheered as though they
were celebrating victory. In fact, it was the heroism of Admiral
David Farragut they were cheering.

Farragut came ashore and was whisked to a reception in his
honor at the Customs House. Afterward, a special committee of
the leading citizens of New York made an official request. "The
citizens of New York can offer no tribute equal to your claim on
their gratitude and affection," read the secretary. "Their earnest
desire is to receive you as one of their number, and to be permitted,
as fellow-citizens, to share in the renown you will bring to the
metropolitan city."

The city gave the outstanding and brave veteran a check for
$50,000 to buy a house in New York. At almost the same time, the
Congress passed a special bill creating the new rank of vice-
admiral, and the next day the title was bestowed on Farragut. In
1866, he was promoted to admiral. Farragut became the first
person in U.S. naval history ever awarded this rank.

The nation's most famous naval hero was glad to be finished
with war work. His health was failing. He tired easily. But there
was still much to do. He was now an icon, a legend among the
people. Fathers told their children stories about the brilliant battles

of Admiral Farragut. Children though of him as a heroic figure from ancient mythology.

All his life David Farragut had kept his obligations; he was used to it. But now his obligation was to attend parties and receptions in his honor. This was harder for him than piloting a vessel. He preferred the simple life of a sailor. But he learned quickly and in time came to enjoy his new role.

There were parties in New York and the surrounding area. Farragut went to Boston to attend a reception in his honor in historic Faneuil Hall. He visited Harvard University, where the students—in honor of their distinguished visitor—unhitched his horses and pulled his carriage through the campus themselves. The old Admiral rode along, laughing.

The week after the Confederacy surrendered, Farragut journeyed south to his old home in Norfolk, Virginia. He had not been to the city since his onetime friends had told him to leave if he supported the North. Now Farragut was sad to find that many people still felt the same. They remembered his parting words: "Mind what I tell you: You fellows will catch the devil before you get through with this business." Farragut had been right. The beaten city did not want to be reminded.

In the summer of 1867 the admiral again put to sea. He was made commander of a special European squadron. On a fine June morning, his flag went up on the steam frigate *Franklin*. This was no ordinary military cruise, however. Farragut's wife was also on board. They were setting off on a round of receptions in his honor being given in all the capitals of Europe.

Before the squadron sailed, Farragut gave a reception aboard the *Franklin*. The deck of the frigate was transformed into an open-air ballroom, with long tables covered with linen tablecloths, magnificent candelabras, and dignified waiters standing by with bottles of fine wine. President Andrew Johnson himself attended the reception. The other ships of the squadron gave a 21-gun salute to the admiral and his guests.

On July 14, 1867, David Farragut dropped anchor in Cherbourg Harbor on the northwest coast of France, on the English Channel, where the *Alabama* had been sunk a few years earlier.

Farragut, now 65 years old, had last been in Europe 47 years earlier when, as an 18-year-old boy, he had received his first promotion, from midshipman to acting lieutenant of the frigate *Shark*.

For the next 16 months Farragut toured the glittering cities of Europe. In Paris he was celebrated by Emperor Napoleon III and Empress Eugenie. Officials in England, France, and Russia asked him to inspect their newly built ironclad fleets.

Despite being an honored guest, Farragut could not help but make military observations about ports, ships, and fortifications. He kept a record of all he saw in his journal, because as he said, "Who knows but that my services may be needed here someday?"

These were his observations of the shipyards in Cherbourg, France: "Cherbourg dockyard is one of the most compact and complete I ever saw. It has nine dry docks. There were four ironclads on the stocks, one being nearly ready for launching. The

Admiral Farragut posed for a photo on board the *Franklin*, during its tour of European capitals.

shops and foundries are in fine order. Saw two steam hammers and two tilt hammers in one shop, 1,000 to 4,000 lbs. each. They put on the iron plating with screws instead of rivets."

In Copenhagen, Farragut was shown a fort and noted: "This fort is made of concrete, molded into shape—that is, it is made in a mold. The effect of a shot upon it would be to mash the part struck, without disintegrating."

In Russia, Farragut was the special guest of Grand Duke Constantine. "Our dinner was a very handsome affair," Farragut wrote. "After the coffee was served, the gypsies sang and danced for us."

The grand duke requested that Farragut visit his fleet. The admiral said he would be happy to accompany the grand duke. But Constantine shook his had. "No," he said, "I want you to go when I am not present, as the honors would be mine, and I wish them to be yours particularly."

Other dinners were given for Farragut by officers of the Russian fleet. One was on board a fine ship. "The dinner went off delightfully," Farragut wrote, "and when we left they burned blue and white lights and cheered lustily."

When the squadron docked in Copenhagen, Farragut looked up two Danish seamen who had befriended him in Tunis when he was a boy living with Reverend Folsom. He was sad to learn that both were now dead. Instead, however, he visited their daughters. He was delighted when one of the daughters showed him a letter written to her father by midshipman David Farragut 50 years earlier. It said, in part:

> "I have also to inform you that this morning, after rising from my bed at eleven o'clock (to my shame), and after mature reflection, I determined to repair immediately to Messina and join the squadron. You may be a little surprised at so sudden a determination, but you know it is the duty of a person in my profession to decide quick, and execute with promptness and spirit.

Admiral Farragut told the woman that he had kept the same quick decisiveness all his life.

In England, Farragut demonstrated that he no longer felt any traces of the anger toward the British that he had felt as a young man in the days following the War of 1812. He was presented to Queen Victoria, and afterward, as a special guest of the Duke of Edinburgh, he mentioned that he had no picture of the Queen. The next day the Duke sent him a framed portrait of the Queen. Farragut was delighted.

The admiral followed the reception by giving a party on board the *Franklin* for English and American sailors. His secretary described the scene:

"The gay decks of the flagship soon became brilliant with glittering uniforms, the dashing scarlet of the English infantrymen contrasting beautifully with the navy blue of the royal artillery and the American line and staff."

In Italy, Farragut and his sailors attended lavish parties. Banquet guests in rich costume took turns saluting one another's country with cries of "Viva America!" and "Viva Italia!"

In Rome, Admiral Farragut had an audience with Pope Pius IX, who said of Farragut, "Of all men, he has a most enviable reputation."

In Spain, Admiral Farragut met Queen Isabella II, who said to him, "I am glad to welcome you to Spain...I am proud to know that your parental ancestors came from my dominions."

One reception in his honor that was most pleasing to the admiral was the one that took place in the town of Ciudadella, on the island of Minorca. This was the birthplace of his father and the home of many of his respected ancestors. In honor of the famous sailor, all work stopped on the day of his arrival. The procession route from Port Mahon to Ciudadella was lined with islanders. In the capital, a band struck up and the mayor and other city officials greeted the admiral. They presented him with a copy of the records showing his father's baptism.

At last, in November 1868, the squadron returned home. It had been a wondrous cruise to cap the admiral's career, but he was glad it was over. His spells of weakness were becoming more frequent. He looked forward to resting.

But others did not let him rest. The government was in a state of confusion. After President Lincoln was assassinated, his vice president, Andrew Johnson, took office. Johnson's administration was troubled by scandals and was unable to heal the wounds of the divided country and guide it into a promising future.

Now a group of politicians approached Farragut. They asked him to allow them to suggest his name as a candidate for the presidency. He was a military hero, a man respected by the people for his courage. He had often demonstrated his ability to plan and carry out complex battles. And he was a winner. They believed he would be a perfect choice.

But Farragut put a quick end to their hopes. "I hasten to assure you that I have never for one moment entertained the idea of political life," he said shortly. And that was that. The country needed a strong leader, he knew, but he was not the man. He was not cut out for politics, and he was too worn out to enter a new career.

Furthermore, Farragut was always cautious, as all good sailors must be. The idea of setting off on such a difficult course so late in life was absurd to him. "My entire life has been spent in the navy," he said. "By a steady perseverance and devotion to it I have been favored with success in my profession, and to risk that reputation by entering a new career at my advanced age, and that career one of which I have little or no knowledge, is more than anyone has a right to expect of me."

So the power brokers looked elsewhere. They soon found the man. Ulysses S. Grant, commander-in-chief of the Union armies, became the Republican candidate for president. He, too, was a war hero, a man known for his strategic ability and courage. Surprisingly, Grant also enjoyed some popularity in the South. After the war he had recommended that the government not impose strict conditions on the South.

Grant was elected president and took office on March 4, 1869. He helped to heal war wounds by declaring amnesty for the leaders of the Confederacy, forgiving them for their actions. Soon, however, he learned that national politics was a more difficult business than war. He had hoped to carve out a path for the country to follow. Though honest, Grant was naive, and his administration became buried in scandals.

Problems in Washington did not affect Admiral Farragut, however. He finished off his official duties by visiting the navy yards in California, then made his way back home. In Chicago, he suffered a heart attack. Though he recovered, he never fully regained his health.

In August 1870, Admiral Farragut sailed to Portsmouth, New Hampshire, to the home of a navy colleague. As the ship came into harbor, he got himself up from his sickbed. Outside, he could hear the guns firing an official salute. Farragut put on his full military dress and went up on deck. He looked up at the flag flying from the mast and said, "It would be well if I died now, in harness."

A short time later the ailing admiral expressed a desire to board an old sloop docked in the harbor. As he strode its deck he turned to an old sailor who was standing nearby and said softly, "This is the last time I shall ever tread the deck of a man-of-war."

It was as if he knew his end was near. On August 14, 1870, at the age of 69, Admiral Farragut died.

The United States government planned a state funeral in New York that was on a scale usually reserved for presidents. The admiral's remains were brought by ship to New York. The day of the funeral, September 30, was declared a holiday. Schools, banks, and businesses were closed. The buildings of the city were draped in black.

A military funeral procession wound through the streets. It included 10,000 soldiers and sailors, as well as cabinet members and other government officials. At its head was President Grant, a man who had known Farragut well and depended on his victories at New Orleans and Mobile Bay to advance his Union armies.

So that the admiral would always be remembered, the United States Congress erected a statute of Farragut in Washington, D.C. The area around it, in the heart of the nation's capital, is now known as Farragut Square.

The man who had led the United States Navy in victorious battle in the Civil War was gone. In his lifetime he had seen enormous advances in shipbuilding technology, but his outlook

The cover of *Harper's Weekly* for October 15, 1870, shows Admiral Farragut's funeral procession.

was always that of a simple sailor. He always said that he had no secrets that brought him victory. He preferred to rely on good men rather than on fancy new equipment. And his approach to sea battles was straightforward. "The more you hurt the enemy the less he will hurt you," he often said. He also liked to say, "The best protection against the enemy's fire is a well-directed fire from our own guns," which is another way of stating the old maxim that "the best defense is a good offense."

But the real key to his success was his passion for the sea and the sailor's life, passions that he held firmly throughout his 58-year naval career. He was the most distinguished naval officer of his day, a man who had led dozens of ships in complex, dangerous battles in which the future of his country was at stake. The simple secret of his success is probably best described in a sentence he once wrote. "I have as much pleasure in running into port in a gale of wind," Farragut said, "as ever a boy did in a feat of skill."

DAVID FARRAGUT

July 5,	**1801**	Born at Stony Point, Tennessee
	1810	Becomes midshipman in the U.S. Navy at age nine
	1812–14	Serves on the *Essex* on its voyages in the War of 1812
	1816–20	Serves in the Mediterranean
	1846–48	Sees action in the Mexican War
	1855	Promoted to captain
	1861	The Civil War begins; Farragut leaves the South and joins the Union navy.
	1862	Wins the Battle of New Orleans, gaining control of the Mississippi River for the North
		Promoted to rear admiral
	1864	Captures Mobile Bay, the last Confederate stronghold on the Gulf Coast
		Leaves the fleet and moves to New York
	1866	Commissioned as the first admiral in the U.S. Navy
	1867–68	Honored on a tour of European capitals
Aug. 14,	**1870**	Dies in Portsmouth, New Hampshire

Selected Sources

FARRAGUT

Barnes, James. *David G. Farragut.* Boston, 1899.

Farragut, Loyall. *The Life of David Glasgow Farragut.* New York, 1879.

Hunt, William H., Secretary of the Navy. *Address on the Occasion of the Unveiling of the Statue of Admiral Farragut in Madison Square, New York, May 25, 1881.* Boston, 1881.

Lewis, Charles Lee. *David Glasgow Farragut.* 2 vols. New York: Dodd, Mead & Co., 1941 & 1943.

Mahan, Alfred. T. *Admiral Farragut.* New York, 1895.

Spears, John Randolph. *David G. Farragut.* Philadelphia: G. W. Jacobs, 1905.

Stevens, William Oliver. *David Glasgow Farragut, Our First Admiral.* New York: Dodd, Mead & Co., 1942.

THE CIVIL WAR

Andrews, J. Cutler. *The North Reports the Civil War.* Pittsburgh: University of Pittsburgh Press, 1985.

Catton, Bruce. *The Civil War.* Boston: Houghton Mifflin, 1960.

Catton, Bruce. *This Hallowed Ground.* New York: Washington Square Press, 1955.

Commager, Henry Steele. *The Blue and the Gray: The Story of the Civil War as Told by Participants.* New York: Fairfax Press, 1982.

DeConde, Alexander. *A History of American Foreign Policy.* New York: Scribners, 1971.

Eaton, Clement. *A History of the Southern Confederacy.* New York: The Free Press, 1954.

Fiske, John. *The Mississippi Valley in the Civil War.* Boston and New York, 1897.

Grant, U.S. *Personal Memoirs.* New York: DaCapo Press, 1983.

Jones, Virgil Carrington. *The Civil War at Sea.* Vols. 2 and 3. New York: Holt, Rinehart & Winston, 1962.

Korn, Jerry. *War on the Mississippi.* New York: Time-Life, 1985.

U.S. Naval War Records Office. *Official Records of the Union and Confederate Navies in the War of the Rebellion.* Washington: Government Printing Office, 1894–1922.

Wilkinson, John. *The Narrative of a Blockade Runner.* New York, 1877.

OTHER

Council on Interracial Books for Children. *Chronicles of American Indian Protest.* Greenwich, Conn.: Fawcett, 1971.

Hagan, Kenneth J., ed. *In Peace and War: Interpretations of American Naval History, 1775-1978.* Westport, Conn.: Greenwood Press, 1978.

Mahan, Alfred T. *Sea Power in Its Relations to the War of 1812.* 2 vols. New York: Haskill House, 1969.

Mahan, Alfred T. *From Sail to Steam: Reflections of Naval Life.* New York: Harper, 1907.

Remini, Robert V. *The Revolutionary Age of Jackson.* New York: Harper & Row, 1976.

Schlesinger, Arthur M., Jr. *The Age of Jackson.* Boston: Little, Brown, 1953.

Tocqueville, Alexis de. *Democracy in America.* 2 vols. Henry Reeve translation, revised by Francis Bowen. New York: Knopf, 1987.

Wiltse, Charles M. *The New Nation: 1800-1845.* New York: Hill and Wang, 1961.

PERIODICALS

Harper's Weekly, May 1862, February 1864

Navy Register, 1861-1866

New York *Herald*, April 1862, August 1863

New York *Times*, April-June, 1862

Suggested Reading

*Adkins, Jan. *Wooden Ship: The Building of a Wooden Sailing Vessel in 1870.* Boston: Houghton Mifflin, 1978.

Beatty, Jerome, Jr. *Blockade!* Garden City, N.Y.: Doubleday, 1971.

Donovan, Frank. *The Ironclads.* New York: A. S. Barnes, 1961.

Dupuy, Trevor Nevitt. *The Military History of the Civil War Naval Actions.* New York: Franklin Watts, 1961.

*Freeman, Fred. *Duel of the Ironclads.* New York: Time-Life, 1969.

Korn, Jerry. *War on the Mississippi.* New York: Time-Life, 1985.

Lawson, Don. *The United States in the Mexican War.* New York: Abelard-Schuman, 1976.

McDonald, Forrest. *The Boys Were Men: The American Navy in the Age of Fighting Sail.* New York: Putnam, 1971.

Marrin, Albert. *1812: The War Nobody Won.* New York: Atheneum, 1985.

*O'Dell, Scott. *The 290.* Boston: Houghton Mifflin, 1976.

Ward, Ralph T. *Steamboats.* Indianapolis: Bobbs-Merrill, 1973.

Wyckoff, James. *Who Really Invented the Submarine?* New York: Putnam, 1965.

*Readers of *David Farragut and the Great Naval Blockade* will find these books particularly readable.

INDEX